BEST OF BRITAIN'S

Steam Railways

A SPECTACULAR JOURNEY THROUGH BRITAIN'S STEAM HERITAGE

Produced by AA Publishing

© AA Media Limited 2004
Reprinted February 2010

Published by AA Publishing (a trading name of AA Media Limited, whose registered office is Fanum House, Basing View, Basingstoke, Hampshire RG21 4EA; registered number 06112600)

A04363

ISBN-10: 0-7495-4212-8
ISBN-13: 978-0-7495-4212-2

A CIP catalogue record for this book is available from the British Library.

The contents of this book are believed correct at the time of printing. Nevertheless, the publishers cannot be held responsible for any errors, omissions or for changes in the details given in this book or for the consequences of any reliance on the information provided by the same. This does not affect your statutory rights. We have tried to ensure accuracy in this book but things do change and we would be grateful if readers would advise us of any inaccuracies they may encounter.

Scanning by MRM Graphics Limited, Buckinghamshire
Printed and bound by Leo Paper Products, China

PICTURE ACKNOWLEDGEMENTS
The Automobile Association wishes to thank the following libraries and photographers for their assistance in the preparation of this book.

Peter C I Adams 12, 12/3; Image Courtesy of Amberley Working Museum 128t, 129tr; Bure Valley Railway Collection 52tc, 56t, 57r; Ian Butters 105; Cornish Picture Library 18bl Paul Watts, 19 David Hastilow; Dart Valley Railway Plc 20, 21t, 144; Paul Davis 60/1; East Somerset Railway/Phil Hamerton 14; John East 62, 64, 65t; Mike Esau 34, 35, 37t; Foxfield Railway 33b/g tr, 53b/g tr, 71b/g tr, 115b/g tr, 129b/g tr, 143b/g tr; Great Central Railway 63; D Hewitt 128b; Simon Hopkins 16t; David Idle 122, 123, 124, 125; Isle of Man Tourism 113; Isle of Wight Steam Railway 39; Peter Johnson 83, 84, 106, 107; KWVR/Dixon Target 52tl, 118t, 118b, 119t; Llanberis Lake Railway 86t, 86b, 87r; Ian Lothian 134, 135, 136, 137; M & G N Joint Railway Society 6/7 Steve Allen, 52tr, 76; Mid-Hants Railway 43t, 43b, 44t; Milepost 92 1/2 4, 6, 8/9, 9, 10, 21b, 22, 23, 32/3b/g, 32b/g tl, 32b/g tr, 32t, 32b, 33b/g tl, 33b/g tc, 33t, 33bl, 33br, 36, 37b, 38, 40, 52b/g tl, 52b/g tr, 52b, 53b/g tl, 53b/g tc, 53b, 54, 55t, 55b, 65b, 66/7, 68, 70b/g tl, 70b/g tr, 70tr, 70b, 71b/g tl, 71b/g tc, 72, 73, 74t, 74br, 75, 82, 88, 89b, 90, 91, 92, 93, 94t, 94b, 95t, 95b, 97, 108, 108/9, 109, 110, 111, 112t, 112br, 114b/g tl, 114b/g tc, 114tl, 115b/g tl, 115b/g tc, 120, 121, 128b/g tl, 128b/g tc, 129b/g tl, 129b/g tc, 129l, 129cr, 140t, 142b/g tl, 142b/g tc, 142tl, 142tc, 142tr, 143b/g tl, 143b/g tc, 143b; Robert Morland 100br; National Railway Museum 114/5, 115c, 115b; Bill Oats 41, 42bl, 42br; Andrew Ponsford 13; Ravenglass & Eskdale Railway/Ken Cservenka 126, 126/7, 127; Bill Roberton 140; Romney Hythe & Dymchurch Railway 48/9, 50, 51t, 51b; Ian Rutherford 59; Andrew Smith 74bl; Frank Spence 88t; Snowdon Mountain Railway 96; Steve Standbridge 16/7; Tanfield Railway 130/1, 132, 133l, 133r;; Mr R Tilley 79t; Vale of Rheidol Railway 102, 103tl; Adrian Vaughan 56/7; David J Williams 29, 30b, 31t, 31b; Andrew P M Wright 24/5, 26t, 26b, 27, 28; Ian Wright 30t; Mr P G Wright 85.

The remaining photographs are held in the AA's own photo library (AA World Travel Library) and were taken by the following photographers:
Pat Aithie 78t, 78b, 79b, 87l; Marius Alexander 134/5; M Alward-Coppin 101; Adrian Baker 117; Vic Bates 112bl; Jeff Beazley 71bl; E A Bowness 138, 139t; Ian Burgum 2, 80, 81, 99; Derek Croucher 142ct, 143t; Steve Day 70tl; R J Edwards 76t, 77tl, 77tr, 77b; Eric Ellington 141b; Derek Forss 139b; Cameron Lees 126/7; S&O Mathews 71tr; Eric Meacher 15tl, 15b; C Molyneaux 81r; Roger Moss front cover, 1, 10/1, 18t, 142b; John Mottershaw 116, 119b; Rich Newton 98, 100bl, 114c; Neil Ray 15tr; Forbes Stephenson 16c; Andy Tryner 58, 69t, 69b; Wyn Voysey 39r, 44b, 45, 46/7.

THE BRECON MOUNTAIN RAILWAY – THE NEAT MAROON 0-6-2T HAILED FROM A PASSENGER LINE IN EAST GERMANY

Contents

Foreword

No one, fifty years ago, could have imagined the extent to which railway preservation would aspire. But the age of steam captured the hearts of millions of people embracing all ages, backgrounds and professions. Steam locomotives had been the driving force of the industrial revolution; they had enabled popular travel and created their own world of magic and intrigue upon which the nation became entirely dependent.

Railway territory was hallowed ground; it was a world set aside from the rest of society; its people invariably came from railway families and the camaraderie had to be experienced to be believed. The railway abounded in glorious architecture and engineering triumphs both civil and mechanical; it permeated all aspects of industry and it scaled the nation's physical barriers. He who understood railways had his finger on the nation's pulse. The railway provided a safe and disciplined transport system at the heart of which was the steam locomotive, a living machine animated by the elemental forces of fire and water.

Britain has some 200 centres at which steam traction can be witnessed and the top 100 of these are celebrated in this volume. Over 2,000 steam locomotives have been preserved along with a magnificent range of rolling stock. And the movement continues apace; in 2004–36 years after the last steam locomotive ran on British Railways—came the news that the former LMS 10 road locomotive depot at Workington was to be systematically dismantled and recreated on the Great Central Railway at Loughborough. That this work is being done in association with Network Rail and the Railway Heritage Trust, makes it doubly inspiring. In addition, the Great Central are aspiring to rebuild the viaduct over the Midland Mainline at Loughborough to facilitate through running from Ruddington on the southern outskirts of Nottingham to Leicester North, a distance of 18 miles. The concept of a double track steam mainline, with trains running at realistic line speeds, linking two large British cities is the stuff of legend; a golden opportunity which has tourist potential of international significance. It is a project in which the vitality of the steam age itself is personified. The possibilities for enthralling future generations on the rich legacy of Britain's railway history are—given the will and determination—endless.

Colin Garratt
Milepost 92½
November 2004

LEFT: FORMER LMS STANIER PACIFIC DUCHESS OF HAMILTON ON THE GREAT CENTRAL RAILWAY.

Introduction

Britain leads the world in railway preservation; a situation appropriate to its history, as the steam locomotive was arguably Britain's greatest technological gift to mankind while Britain financed, built, exported and operated a vast amount of overseas railways.

The animation and excitement of steam railways has always been a magnet for people of every age and background. As recently as 50 years ago it seemed impossible that the steam locomotive could ever disappear; it was the prime motive force of the railway and the railway was the heartbeat of the nation. If the railway stopped, Britain stopped, in those years when Britain's transport was primarily in the hands of 25,000 steam locomotives.

Under the government's Railway Modernisation Plan of 1955, steam traction was to be phased out and along with

RIGHT: THE FORMER LNER B12 CLASS 4-6-0 NO. 61572 ROMPS THROUGH THE NORFOLK COUNTRYSIDE BETWEEN SHERINGHAM AND WEYBOURNE WITH ITS LIGHTWEIGHT TRAIN.

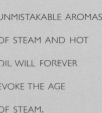

LEFT: THE UNMISTAKABLE AROMAS OF STEAM AND HOT OIL WILL FOREVER EVOKE THE AGE OF STEAM.

Britain's Best Steam Railways

the dying steam locomotive came a massive programme of line closures under the Beeching Report. While Beeching's actions were a disaster for the nation, they did release a wide variety of branch and secondary lines, many in scenic areas frequented by tourists. The government's idea for the preservation of our steam heritage was to save a select number of locomotives to keep on static display. But to the tens of thousands of railway enthusiasts life without steam railways was greeted with dismay. So began the dynamic movement to save steam locomotives and rolling stock from the breaker's torch and to take over redundant parts of the railway network which had been closed. The movement went from strength to strength and in its

RIGHT: THE FORMER TAFF VALE RAILWAY 0-6-2T NO. 85 IS AT THE CENTRE OF THIS GROUP OF LOCOMOTIVES IN REPOSE ON THE KEIGHLEY & WORTH VALLEY RAILWAY.

BELOW: THE POWER AND THE GLORY OF STEAM ON THE MAIN LINE IS EXEMPLIFIED BY LMS PACIFIC *DUCHESS OF HAMILTON* HARD AT WORK AGAINST THE MAJESTIC SETTING OF THE PENNINE HILLS.

formative years was almost entirely run by volunteers with financial backing and help in kind coming from a wide variety of sources including local authorities.

Railway preservationists have bequeathed to the nation a leading tourist attraction which is now so ingrained in the national psyche that many foreign visitors regard a journey on a steam train as synonymous with a visit to Britain.

Quite apart from providing both education and recreation, preserved lines do much to promote interest in the railway itself, not least 'Days out with Thomas' which offer youngsters a dramatic introduction to the railway. And it is essential that the coming generations are educated to know and love railways. These are worrying times for corporate railway industry; rail has enemies—both with and without vested interests—and there are those in high places who would contend that railways are an outmoded form of technology. It is known within the railway industry that Beeching's closures would have been much worse had there not been influential people who cared passionately about the industry and who deflected some of his ideas.

The need for youngsters to be involved with railways affects the preserved lines too. As the cost of maintaining the increasingly obsolete and specialised machinery, along with all the related infrastructure, becomes ever higher, the volunteer element will be a major factor in survival. Few preserved railways today have the volunteers they need. The future is unpredictable; hopefully the magnificent railways featured in this book will become increasingly linked with the national network and enable Britain's social, industrial and technological history to be better understood. At worst, many of these lines could end up on the scrapheap from which they were valiantly rescued. Enjoy them now for they are truly a miracle.

ABOVE: GREAT WESTERN LOCOMOTIVES, WITH THEIR COPPER AND BRASSWORK, CALL FOR DEDICATED VOLUNTEERS TO PRESENT THEM AT THEIR BEST.

Bodmin & Wenford Railway
Cornwall
Bodmin, 16 miles (25km) west of Liskeard

The Bodmin & Wenford Railway offers a unique opportunity to compare the most modern of rail services with the nostalgia of the age of steam. It is the only preserved railway that is served by 125mph (200kph) High Speed Trains, and after being whisked from London Paddington or Edinburgh, passengers can cross a covered footbridge at Bodmin Parkway to an island platform from which Bodmin & Wenford trains depart. The 6½mile (10.5km) line, originally opened by the Great Western Railway in 1887, is the only standard gauge preserved railway in Cornwall, and recalls the days when the county was served by a fine network of picturesque branch lines to many of the principal resorts and market towns.

As the branch line turns away from the main line, it crosses a five-arch viaduct across the River Fowey, which rises on Bodmin Moor, then begins a taxing climb through

wooded cuttings towards the one intermediate stop at Colesloggett Halt. This was built by the Bodmin & Wenford to serve a network of paths created by the Forestry Commission through nearby Cardinham Woods.

The climb continues on a gradient of about 1 in 40 through banks of bracken and foxgloves with fine views over the surrounding countryside and to Bodmin Moor. On the outskirts of Bodmin you pass the FitzGerald Lighting factory and sidings of stored railway vehicles. A Historic Carriage Restoration Building is expected to be built on this area in 2005. Next we pass the redundant barracks of the Duke of Cornwall's Light Infantry. In 1944 the railway carried Field Marshall Montgomery and General Eisenhower during the D-Day preparations.

As the train enters Bodmin General station after the 25-minute slog uphill (it only takes 20 minutes going down) we can see the line to Boscarne going out to the left. Bodmin General is the railway's headquarters and has two large locomotive sheds, one of which is usually open to the public. The terminus building houses a gift shop, buffet, toilets and waiting room. You can hire cycles at the station; they are carried free on the train.

The loco is taken off the train here and runs round to the other end ready for the downhill journey to Boscarne Junction, 3 miles away. Boscarne Junction is where the Great Western line met the Bodmin & Wadebridge Railway route from Padstow and Wadebridge to Bodmin and Wenford. The old track bed now forms the Camel Trail footpath and cycleway. There are plans to relay the railway initially to Grogley Halt, but eventually all the way to a new station in the south of Wadebridge.

TRAIN SERVICE

DAILY, EASTER, JUNE TO SEPTEMBER; SELECTED DATES MARCH, APRIL, MAY, OCTOBER, NOVEMBER. FULL TIMETABLE INCLUDES DETAILS OF THE FIRST CLASS DINING COACH SPECIALS, EVENING MURDER MYSTERY ALSO STEAM, BEER AND JAZZ SPECIALS AND GOODS BRAKEVAN TRIPS. *THOMAS* VISITS THE RAILWAY END OF JULY. SANTA SPECIALS AND MINCE PIE RAMBLERS OPERATE ON CERTAIN DATES IN DECEMBER.

TEL: 0845 1259678

WEBSITE: WWW.BODMINANDWENFORDRAILWAY.CO.UK

Dean Forest Railway
Gloucestershire
Lydney, 9 miles (14.5km) northeast of Chepstow

centre and has a low level station terminus and a high level platform on the Parkend line.

That simple description belies the Herculean task of its creation on the site of a colliery that once employed 400 men. By the time the Dean Forest Railway began work, both colliery and railway were returning to the forest, calling for labouring on a scale seldom equalled in preservation. All buildings had disappeared, so every structure has had to be located, bought, dismantled, transported and re-erected: a signal box from Gloucester, a platform from Chippenham, a station building from

Coal and iron ore have been mined in the Forest of Dean since before Roman times. By the late 18th century crude waggon-ways were being built to transport the minerals out of the forest, and some of these were later converted into steam-worked railways. The line of the Dean Forest Railway was one of them. It started as a horse-drawn tramroad in 1810, built by the Severn & Wye Railway, and was gradually converted to steam traction and railway standards. The 4-mile (7km) section operated by the Dean Forest Railway is the last of innumerable lines into the forest, and runs from Lydney Junction to Norchard, Whitecroft and Parkend. Norchard hosts the main

RIGHT: A VISITOR TO THE DFR IN THE SHAPE OF
FORMER PORT TALBOT RAILWAY 0-6-0ST NO. 813
WHEELS ITS TRAIN ROUND THE SHARP CURVES THAT
ABOUND BETWEEN NORCHARD AND WHITECROFT.

deeper in the forest. Equally, the Dean Forest's engines have had to be restored from a dire condition. The core of the present fleet consists of ex-Great Western Pannier Tanks and a small Prairie Tank, all three resurrected from the scrapyard at Barry.

Trains edge north into the thickly wooded valley above Norchard, cross the Lyd on a rebuilt skew girder bridge, climb through Whitecroft and enter Forestry Commission land and then Parkend. Trains are about to reach this tranquil village railhead which has already been rebuilt. Plans are in hand to extend farther into the old Coleford Junction yard to provide more convenient access to Cannop Ponds and the Speech House.

The Dean Forest Railway prides itself on the Royal Forester First Class Dining Train which runs fortnightly, and their Branchline Experience Courses. Day-course members drive, fire, and operate crossing gates, signal boxes and brakevans. Quite apart from visiting a wonderful railway in a delightful setting, the Dean Forest puts on many special events. See the website for details.

TRAIN SERVICE

SUNDAYS FROM APRIL TO OCTOBER; ALSO WEDNESDAYS AND SATURDAYS JUNE TO SEPTEMBER; THURSDAYS IN AUGUST; PLUS BANK HOLIDAYS IN SEASON AND SANTA SPECIALS IN DECEMBER.

24-HOUR INFORMATION LINE: 01594 843423

WEBSITE: WWW.DEANFORESTRAILWAY.CO.UK

East Somerset Railway

Somerset

Cranmore, 2 miles (3km) east of Shepton Mallet

TRAIN SERVICE

ALL YEAR ON SELECTED DAYS. A RANGE OF SPECIAL EVENTS IS OPERATED BY THE EAST SOMERSET RAILWAY.

TEL: 01749 880417

WEBSITE: WWW.EASTSOMERSETRAILWAY.COM

Most preserved railways are the result of a shared vision which drives widely different people to pool their skills. The East Somerset Railway, however, was the brainchild of just one man – and he holds elephants responsible. In 1967 the wildlife painter David Shepherd had just sold all his paintings of elephants on exhibition in New York when the opportunity arose to indulge his other passion – steam railways – by buying one of British Rail's last steam locomotives. Naturally he needed somewhere to keep it, along with the other locomotives he was later to acquire, and this 2-mile (3km) line is the result of a long search.

The main station is at Cranmore, where there is a connection with Network Rail through a line that was once part of the Great Western Railway branch from Witham to Yatton via Shepton Mallet and Wells, though today it is used only for stone traffic. The station building at Cranmore is the only remaining original station on the entire branch, though the signal box, of a later date, has survived and is currently undergoing restoration to bring it back into full service. At Cranmore, there is also an art gallery displaying David Shepherd's work.

The lush pastures and woods through which the line passes, is home to badgers, foxes and deer, and the deep Doulting Cutting abounds with ancient fossils, for which it has been designated a Site of Special Scientific Interest.

The 35-minute round trip can be broken at the halt provided for picnickers at Merryfield Lane on the outward journey, or at Cranmore West on the return. The halt here enables you to walk through the marvellous replica of a Great Western Railway engine shed and admire the well-equipped workshops from a viewing platform. It's here that the East Somerset's steam locomotives are overhauled. They range from a Great Western Railway Class 56XX, to the tiny industrial tanks, *Lord Fisher* and *Lady Nan*, and include a rare Crane Tank from a steelworks in Staffordshire. You can also watch as the volunteers restore a rare E1 and a USA Tank locomotive. The East Somerset Railway is proud of its reputation as a welcoming and friendly place to visit.

LEFT: The signal box at Cranmore.

RIGHT: The imposing air-smoothed shape of SR Bulleid Light Pacific no. 34105 Swanage.

BELOW: The small industrial locomotive Andrew Barclay 0-4-0ST Lady Nan.

Gloucestershire & Warwickshire Railway

Gloucestershire

Toddington, 7 miles (11.5km) northeast of Cheltenham

The Gloucestershire & Warwickshire Railway (the other GWR) started with nothing more than a trackless railway route, with few surviving buildings between Broadway and Cheltenham Racecourse. It has already re-opened 10 miles (16km) of the line, and its ultimate goal is to run all the way to Stratford-upon-Avon, where the line originally met the surviving commuter route to Birmingham. To rebuild the existing line between the headquarters at Toddington and Cheltenham Racecourse, volunteers have rebuilt platforms, dismantled all manner of buildings and artefacts for re-erection and set up facilities for the repair and maintenance of locomotives and carriages. Cheltenham Racecourse Station was reopened on 7th April 2003 and in the same year the GWR won the Ian Allan Independent Railway of the Year award.

Before leaving on the 90-minute journey, passengers can visit Toddington station's 2ft (600mm) gauge North Gloucestershire Railway offering rides behind a German engine.

The route of the GWR. runs south from Toddington through the picturesque Vale of Evesham, awash with apple and fruit blossom in spring. The produce of the orchards had been a major source of traffic for the railway, which was closed by British Rail in 1977. Running parallel with the line to the east is the Cotswold escarpment, its limestone providing the lovely honey-coloured stone that is used in local buildings.

BELOW: ATTACHING A HEADLAMP ON A GWR LOCOMOTIVE AT TODDINGTON.
RIGHT: A GREAT WESTERN 'HALL' CLASS 4-6-0 ON ITS WAY TO CHELTENHAM RACECOURSE.

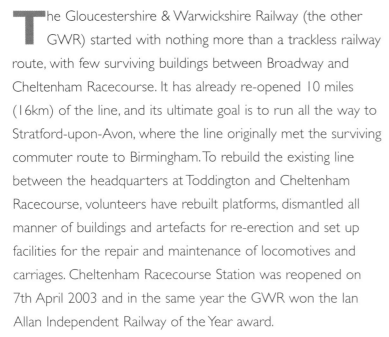

TRAIN SERVICE

STEAM: WEEKENDS AND SOME SUMMER WEEKDAYS FROM END MARCH TO OCTOBER, SUNDAYS ONLY IN NOVEMBER; ALSO DIESEL ON SELECTED DAYS. ELEGANT EXCUSIONS – WINE AND DINE TRAINS – RUN ON SELECTED DAYS ALONG WITH SANTA AND OTHER FAMILY SPECIALS.

TEL: 01242 621405

WEBSITE: WWW.GWSR.COM

In the area of the ridge are the remains of the 13th-century Hailes Abbey, once served by a halt on the railway. Beyond Didbrook the observant eye can discern remnants of the medieval strip farming, denoted by rectangles of raised ground.

Winchcombe station building stood at Monmouth (Troy) until it was dismantled and each stone numbered to assist re-erection. As the train pulls away, it enters the cutting leading to Greet Tunnel which, at 693yds (633m) is the second longest on a preserved railway. The line skirts the south side of Dickston Hill in a deep cutting re-emerging a short distance before Gotherington Station. The track decends 1.5 miles (2.5km) to the villages of Woodmancote and Bishop's Cleeve before curving gently right into Cheltenam Racecourse Station which lies in a picturesque cutting. The original station waiting room/ticket office can only just be seen from the platforms as it is positioned high above the track bed at road level.

Launceston Steam Railway
Cornwall
Launceston, 10 miles (16km) west of Tavistock

The tranquil countryside of north Cornwall may seem a strange place to see at work a collection of enchanting narrow gauge locomotives that spent their working lives in the slate quarries of north Wales. Their presence here is the result of the encouraging response given by the local authority to the idea of building a railway for them on the trackbed of the line that once carried the Atlantic Coast Express.

Opened in stages since 1983, the Launceston Steam Railway offers a 2-mile (3km) journey along the broad valley of the River Kensey. It is skilful in bringing together of buildings and fixtures from far and wide. The café and booking hall was originally a three-bedroom bungalow at Cranleigh in Surrey that had been on show at the first Ideal Home Exhibition in 1919, and sheltering passengers on the platform outside is the canopy from nearby Tavistock North station. The adjacent large stone building was once used by the Launceston Gas Company. Its ground floor is now the British Engineering Exhibition, housing stationary steam engines. One of the engines here was used by a hospital near Hitchin to drive water pumps and laundry machinery. Above the engines, reached by a staircase rescued from New Cross Hospital in London, is a collection of vintage cars and motorcycles.

The tall-funnelled quarry engines are all centenarians and products of Hunslet in Leeds. They amble along, taking 40 minutes for the round trip, although visitors can stop off at Hunts Crossing for a picnic beside the river – courtesy of the kind farmer who owns the field. The area is a haven for wildlife, and passengers may be lucky enough to see herons, woodpeckers and buzzards, while the railway banks are known to be home to stoats, badgers, lizards, and grass snakes.

TRAIN SERVICE

DAILY EXCEPT SATURDAYS FROM WHITSUN UNTIL
SEPTEMBER. TUESDAYS AND SUNDAYS FROM EASTER
AND IN OCTOBER.

TEL: 01566 775665

Beyond Hunts Crossing the valley
opens up, affording wider views over the
farmland. The line stops at New Mills
where passengers can explore the
footpaths in the valley or visit the Farm
Park alongside the station. Always
popular with children, the park is a
separate attraction. Looking farther along
the overgrown route, it is hard to
imagine the holiday expresses packed
with excited holidaymakers which once
rushed through the valley on their way
from London Waterloo and Exeter to
Wadebridge and Padstow.

When workers were excavating the
railway cutting in Launceston they
discovered the buried remains of the
1,000-year-old priory which had been
forgotten since it was destroyed by
Henry VIII in 1539. Recent land purchases
by the Steam Railway enable visitors to
view the ruin, while displays of historical
material help to unravel the mystery of
one of the strangest areas imaginable.
Narrow gauge engines now run over
tracks laid through the cloisters and the
nave where monks once prayed.

Paignton & Dartmouth Steam Railway

Devon

Paignton, 3 miles (5km) north of Torquay

Dartmouth Steam Railway begins amid the candyfloss of Paignton town centre, runs along the cliffs overlooking Torbay before turning inland for a mile or two of pastoral Devon, and then the line drops down to sea level beside the wooded estuary of the River Dart.

This line was once part of Brunel's broad gauge (7ft/2.13m) Great Western Railway, leaving the West of England main line to the south of Newton Abbot station and serving Torquay en route. After conversion to standard gauge, it became the destination of the Torbay Express from London Paddington, but the final 7 miles (11.5km) no longer provided the required financial returns. It was closed in 1972, only to be reopened in the same year by an offshoot of the Dart Valley Railway.

At Paignton the lines of the National Railway network had to be separated from the Paignton & Dartmouth, although through excursion trains can still be transferred and the interchange between the two is very easy. The trains of the Paignton & Dartmouth still evoke the character of the Great Western, with its Middle Green locomotives and chocolate-and-cream coaches, although most of the carriages are of later manufacture. The steep gradients of the line mean that powerful locomotives have to be used except during the quieter parts of the year.

All the railway's steam engines are of GWR ancestry. The most powerful is a heavy tank locomotive built originally for south Wales coal trains. No 5239, named *Goliath* by the Paignton & Dartmouth, was built in 1924 and rescued from a

TRAIN SERVICE

SELECTED DATES APRIL, MAY AND OCTOBER; DAILY FROM MAY TO SEPTEMBER. SANTA SPECIALS.

TEL: 01803 555872

WEBSITE: WWW.PAIGNTON-STEAMRAILWAY.CO.UK

huge collection of locomotives stored for scrap at Barry in south Wales. In the event, only a handful were cut up; the majority were bought for use on preserved railways. Many were badly corroded and missing vital parts, and their return to service is a tribute to the tenacity and skill of volunteers and the few paid engineers on railways all over Britain.

One tender locomotive, No 7827 *Lydham Manor*, was rescued from Barry, but one of two 45XX class tank engines, No 4555, was bought while still in service on British Railways. Other small tank engines are unlikely to be seen on service trains as they are too underpowered for the steep gradients that are apparent soon after leaving Paignton.

The journey starts by travelling past what is left of Goodrington carriage sidings. After crossing the stone viaducts at Broadsands and Hookhills, the line begins to run inland, pausing at Churston before beginning its descent to the sea via the 497-yard (454m) Greenway Tunnel, one of the longest on a preserved railway. As the train bursts out of the tunnel, you get your first glimpse of the river and hundreds of tiny boats as the train drops down from the curve of Greenway Viaduct.

A range of tickets is available for the half-hour single journey, so that passengers can take the ferry across the harbour or include an excursion on the River Dart.

FAR LEFT: GREAT WESTERN 2-8-0T NO. 5239 BRINGS A HEAVYWEIGHT TRAIN HEADED BY THE DEVON BELLE OBSERVATION CAR ALONGSIDE THE RIVER DART.

ABOVE: GWR 'SMALL PRAIRIE' TANK NO. 4588 WITH TORBAY IN THE BACKGROUND.

LEFT: NO. 4588 PASSES GOODRINGTON SANDS.

South Devon Railway
Devon
Buckfastleigh, adjacent to A38 Devon Expressway

TRAIN SERVICE

DAILY FROM EARLY APRIL TO THE END OF OCTOBER, DECEMBER SANTA-BY-STEAM.

TEL: 0845 3451466

WEBSITE: WWW.SOUTHDEVONRAILWAY.ORG

The line, originally built by the South Devon Railway, is seldom out of view of the River Dart during the 25-minute journey. It is one of the prettiest stretches of the river valley and can be appreciated to the full only from the train, since few roads thread the valley and glimpses of the river from the road are rare. The water is home to salmon and trout, so the lucky passenger might catch sight of a salmon leaping its way up-river to spawn. Flying over the water you may see ducks, swans, herons or even a kingfisher, and beside the line is a profusion of primroses and wild daffodils in spring. If time permits, alight at the lovely intermediate station at Staverton. From here, as from Totnes station, there are pleasant walks along the river. The line appears in many TV and cinema films.

In common with other tourist railways in the West Country, the South Devon Railway relies upon holidaymakers for most of its traffic, but no other line began its second life in the way that this one did. The railway was set up by a group of businessmen who believed that the former Great Western Railway branch line from Totnes to Ashburton could be run as a commercial enterprise, and that a volunteer workforce would not be crucial to its operation. This soon proved to be false and today the South Devon Railway is a charity and is operated mainly by volunteer labour.

The line north of Buckfastleigh disappeared with the construction of the A38 Devon Expressway in 1969, so Buckfastleigh is now the northern terminus of the branch. Most passengers join trains here. The station is easy to reach from the A38, has a large car park and is handy for attractions in the area. But Totnes has much to recommend it too, and the SDR terminus, with its footbridge over the River Dart, is close to the mainline station and town centre.

LEFT: GWR 0-4-2T NO. 1420 ALONGSIDE THE TUMBLING WATERS OF THE RIVER DART.

RIGHT: 2251 CLASS 0-6-0 GOODS LOCOMOTIVE UNDER THE FOOTBRIDGE AT BUCKFASTLEIGH.

Swanage Railway

Dorset

Swanage, 10 miles (16km) south of Bournemouth

The existence of the Swanage Railway, one of Britain's most attractive steam railways, represents a triumph of local opinion over the recommendations of the district council. The council had acquired the site for redevelopment, but before their plans were put into action, they decided to ask the inhabitants of the seaside town whether they would prefer the station to reopen. The townspeople voted overwhelmingly in favour of the station, and so began the reconstruction of the picturesque branch that had opened up the previously remote Isle of Purbeck in 1885.

The line has gradually been rebuilt from Swanage, through Harman's Cross and the famous village of Corfe Castle and on to the present terminus at Norden. Today it not only provides a delightful journey through the Purbeck countryside, but also helps to relieve pressure on the traffic-choked village of Corfe Castle and the busy town of Swanage. Most of the railway buildings had survived, though the tracks had to be relaid, and because the bridges along the line were designed to carry heavy express locomotives – Swanage once

TRAIN SERVICES

MOST WEEKENDS THROUGHOUT THE YEAR. DAILY FROM APRIL TO THE END OF OCTOBER. SANTA SPECIALS IN DECEMBER.

TEL: **01929 425800**

WEBSITE: WWW.SWANAGERAILWAY.CO.UK

LEFT: LIKE SUMMER SATURDAYS IN THE 1950s–SWANAGE RAILWAY PUTS ON A SHOW FOR VISITORS.

had an express service to London Waterloo – its trains are once again hauled by such large locomotives as a Bulleid Light Pacific.

Swanage station has been wonderfully restored to its 1930s appearance, from the colour of the paintwork on its period buildings to its enamel advertising signs, and the increasingly rare sight of semaphore signals contribute to the atmosphere. It takes about 45 minutes for the 6-mile (9.5km) journey to Norden, but most travellers break the trip somewhere along the way, either to visit Corfe Castle, with its stirring Civil War history and evocative castle ruins, or to enjoy one of the fine walks around Purbeck, particularly on the escarpment to the north which is rich in early remains. Iron Age Badbury Rings fort is just 12 miles (19km) north.

TOP LEFT: 'THOMAS THE TANK ENGINE' EVENTS HELP TO ENCOURAGE A NEW GENERATION OF YOUNGSTERS TO TAKE A PRACTICAL INTEREST IN RAILWAYS.

LEFT: A BULLEID LIGHT PACIFIC HAULS ITS TRAIN PAST PICNICKERS NEAR CORFE CASTLE.

RIGHT: TURNING SWANAGE TURNTABLE REQUIRES MUSCLE POWER.

West Somerset Railway
Somerset
Bishops Lydeard, 5 miles (8km) northwest of Taunton

Stretching for 20 miles (32km) between Bishops Lydeard and Minehead, the West Somerset Railway is the longest preserved railway in Britain. It may one day be even longer, for there is still a connection with the main line to the west of Taunton station for the occasional through excursion. For the time being, however, passengers arriving by train at Taunton are usually met by a connecting bus which takes them to the eastern terminus at Bishops Lydeard.

The existence of this railway is due to the initiative of the county council, which purchased the line following its closure by British Rail in 1971. This enabled the West Somerset Railway to refurbish the route and reopen it between 1976 and 1979. It retains the atmosphere of a Great Western Railway single-track holiday branch – indeed it became so busy during the summer months that two special passing loops had to be built to break up sections between stations, and the platform at Minehead was lengthened to accommodate 16-coach trains. This legacy has stood West Somerset Railway in good stead, for it needs to run long trains during the peak holiday season to cope with the number of travellers. Passengers at Bishops Lydeard have plenty to occupy their time, as there is a visitor centre in the former

TRAIN SERVICE

MOST DAYS BETWEEN EASTER AND OCTOBER, DAILY FROM JUNE–SEPTEMBER.

TEL: 01643 707650/704996

WEBSITE: WWW.WEST-SOMERSET-RAILWAY.CO.UK

LEFT: THIS WAS RESCUED FROM BARRY SCRAPYARD IN WALES.

RIGHT: SMALL PRAIRIE TANK NO. 4561.

LEFT: FOOTPLATEMAN'S
BACON AND EGG
BREAKFAST SERVED
ON A SHOVEL FROM
THE FIREBOX.

BELOW: ONE RAILWAY
TRADITION IS THAT THE
SIGNAL BOX IS KEPT
SPOTLESSLY CLEAN.

goods shed, incorporating a locomotive or coach, a working signal box and signals, photographs, railway memorabilia and a model railway.

Northbound trains have a stiff climb for 4 miles (6.5km) to the highest point of the line at Crowcombe Heathfield, where the station has two platforms and a separate stationmaster's house with decorative bargeboards. Views of the Quantock and Brendon Hills open up to the left before arrival at Stogumber, an example of minimalist station design, with its tiny platform shelter. At this station passengers can take advantage of a picnic site in lovely surroundings. The half-way station of Williton has two architectural delights for connoisseurs of industrial buildings: the only surviving operational Bristol & Exeter Railway signal box; and a very early metal-framed prefabricated structure dismantled at Swindon railway works and re-erected here. A listed building, it now accommodates rolling stock.

Beyond Williton the train comes within 15yds (13.5m) of the sea at high tide, and as it approaches Watchet station it skirts the harbour on the right. Still active with commercial shipping up to 2,500 tonnes, Watchet is the oldest port in the county and has recently celebrated its millennium. It was the prime reason for the arrival of the railway in 1862. The extension to Minehead took another 12 years to complete. It was in the docks at Watchet that Coleridge is believed to have found inspiration for *The Rime of the Ancient Mariner* in his conversations with sailors. Energetic passengers equipped for walking can leave the train here, or at the next station, Washford, to explore the remains of the West Somerset Mineral Railway. This line was built primarily to convey iron ore extracted from the Brendon Hills to Watchet harbour for shipment across the Bristol Channel to the foundries of south Wales. The most interesting part is the section from Comberow, where an inclined plane ascended the slope of the hills.

Leaving Watchet the line turns inland and crosses the trackbed of the mineral railway before reaching Washford, where a small museum commemorates the Somerset & Dorset Railway, a route which once ran through the Mendips from Bath to Bournemouth. The line returns to the sea as it nears Blue Anchor, where the waiting room houses a museum of GWR artefacts. With marvellous views out to sea, the line hugs the shore to Dunster. A break in the 1-hour-20-minute journey to walk up the road to this attractive and interesting village is strongly recommended.

A long straight takes the railway past the largest holiday centre in the country and into the terminus and headquarters of the railway, where locomotives and carriages are repaired. Beyond are Old Minehead and the 17th-century harbour.

LEFT: THE WSR IS POPULAR WITH FILM AND TV COMPANIES REQUIRING HISTORIC RAILWAY SEQUENCES.

BELOW: IN KEEPING WITH THE SPIRIT OF THE STEAM RAILWAY, WSR PASSENGERS AT TAUNTON ARE TAKEN TO BISHOP'S LYDEARD STATION IN CLASSIC BUSES AND COACHES.

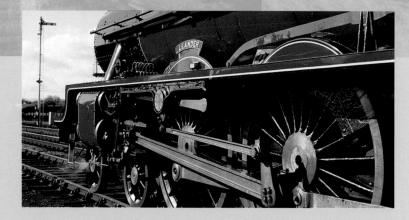

Main Line Steam Operations

ABOVE: LMS JUBILEE CLASS NO. 5690 *LEANDER*.

LEFT: UNDER THE ELEGANT CURVING ROOF OF YORK STATION, SOUTHERN RAILWAY 4-6-0 NO. 850 *LORD NELSON* STANDS READY TO HAUL THE SCARBOROUGH SPA EXPRESS.

There was a time in the early 1970s, when the last years of steam locomotives on main line railways were a recent memory. Their use on special trains was prohibited, except for one engine – Flying Scotsman. An earlier agreement between British Rail and the famous locomotive's owner, Alan Pegler, allowed it to run several excursions, including the epic non-stop run from London to Edinburgh which the BBC made into a fine documentary.

The arrival of Sir Richard Marsh as Chairman of British Rail in 1971 heralded a complete turnaround, and it was accepted that British Rail was losing both goodwill and revenue. The return to the main line of some of the many large steam locomotives in private hands was a milestone. Some of these engines were unsuitable for use on lightly engineered preserved railways, and there is a huge difference between the spectacle of an express train of a dozen coaches hurtling along on a main line and the typical preserved railway train of half the length ambling through the countryside.

For two decades now private steam locomotives have been giving pleasure to millions, and adding millions to British Rail's accounts. It hasn't all been plain sailing, of course – stringent and sometimes costly safety checks had to be made by inspectors on a regular basis, and all the trappings of the steam age had been ripped out with great haste, so water columns or hydrants, coaling arrangements and turning facilities or even turntables had to be organised. To simplify matters selected routes were approved for steam running, with one-off exceptions to mark a special anniversary. The most popular have been the famous Settle & Carlisle line and the equally lovely route between Fort William and Mallaig. The latter has proved so popular that regular daily trains have run during the summer months since 1984.

Excursions are organised by different societies. There is no central marketing for steam specials and the only way to find out about all the various special trains is to check the pages of one of the monthly railway magazines with a bent towards steam. Although the steam sections are in relatively rural parts of the country, most excursions start behind electric or diesel power from a major city.

ABOVE: THE *FLYING SCOTSMAN* IN ACTION ON THE
SETTLE AND CARLISLE LINE OVER THE PENNINES.
RIGHT: THE LNER A4 PACIFIC NAMED AFTER ITS
DESIGNER SIR NIGEL GRESLEY.

FAR RIGHT: LMS
PACIFIC *DUCHESS OF
HAMILTON*.

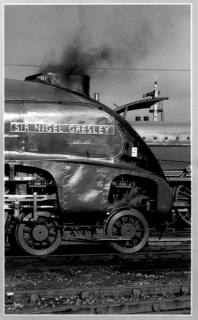

Usually there are good opportunities for passengers to admire the
engine as it takes water, though the frequency of service on most lines
has so far made it impossible to organise on a regular basis the run-
pasts which are a normal part of such occasions in the United States.
These are scrupulously organised events, in which photographers can
leave the train, which then backs down the line under instruction from
organisers with radios. At a given signal, the locomotive accelerates the
train past the photographers, who are tidily lined up to give everyone
a clear view. It then backs down to pick them up before proceeding
on its way. Most of the locomotives with main line certificates are
based at working museums, or on a preserved railway, so they can be
seen at other times.

Bluebell Railway

East Sussex

Sheffield Park, 15 miles (24km) northeast of Brighton

TRAIN SERVICE

WEEKENDS THROUGHOUT THE YEAR, BUT DAILY FROM MAY TO SEPTEMBER AND ON LOCAL SCHOOL HOLIDAYS.

TEL: 01825 720800 FOR GENERAL ENQUIRIES AND 01825 722370 FOR THE TALKING TIMETABLE.

WEBSITE: WWW.BLUEBELL-RAILWAY.CO.UK

ABOVE: THE SPLENDIDLY EQUIPPED WORKSHOPS OF THE BLUEBELL RAILWAY ARE CAPABLE OF PERFORMING THE HEAVIEST OVERHAULS AND RESTORATION WORK ON STEAM LOCOMOTIVES.

RIGHT: E4 CLASS 0-6-2T NO. 473 *BIRCH GROVE* AMID SPRINGTIME BLUEBELLS.

It is little wonder that the Bluebell Railway is probably the best-known preserved railway in Britain. Reopened in 1960, it is the oldest of the former British Railways lines to be saved by preservationists – and one of its engines, *Stepney*, was used as the basis of an engine character by the Reverend W Awdry in his popular children's books. Even those who have not heard of the Bluebell may recognise its southern terminus, since it is named after the nearby National Trust garden of Sheffield Park.

It is worth spending some time at Sheffield Park, admiring the superbly overhauled and repainted locomotives turned out by the well-equipped workshops, and looking at the small museum and model railway on the platform opposite the entrance. The location of the signal box on the platform allows visitors to appreciate the burnished brass instruments and steel levers at closer quarters than most preserved railways.

Having been first in the field, the Bluebell was at a great advantage when it came to buying both locomotives and carriages from British Rail. Steam traction still had eight years to run on Britain's national railways so there were over 10,000 locomotives and hundreds of different classes from which to choose. No railway can rival the Bluebell for the variety and antiquity of its coaches – many date from before World War I and few were built after the second. To sit in a beautifully upholstered compartment, surrounded by polished wood, ornate brass fittings and prints of rail destinations is one of the particular pleasures of a journey on the line.

Another hallmark of the Bluebell is attention to detail when it comes to authenticity, for few railways have been as meticulous in the way stations or rolling stock have been restored. The correct colours are scrupulously applied, and a journey from Sheffield Park takes passengers on something of a trip through time: this station has been renovated in the style of the London Brighton & South Coast Railway which built the line, opening in 1882; Horsted Keynes exemplifies a Southern Railway country junction of the 1930s; and the northern terminus at Kingscote, reopened in 1994 as part of the drive to rejoin the main line at East Grinstead, is being renovated to the style of the 1950s. The journey also takes you from the eastern hemisphere to the west, crossing the line of the Greenwich Meridian as you leave Sheffield Park.

The train accelerates past the elegant starting signal at Sheffield Park so that the locomotive can get to grips with the

FAR LEFT: AFTER A LONG AND COLOURFUL WORKING LIFE, LSWR ADAMS 'RADIAL' TANK NO. 488 HAS AN ACTIVE RETIREMENT ON THE BLUEBELL RAILWAY.
LEFT: WILLIAM STROUDLEY'S BRIGHTON TERRIERS FEATURE PROMINENTLY ON BLUEBELL TRAINS.

BELOW: ONE OF HARRY WAINWRIGHT'S HANDSOME LOCOMOTIVES.

steep 2-mile (3km) climb up Freshfield Bank. The woods that follow give the railway its name, for in May they are a mass of bluebells, almost irridescent in dappled spring sunshine. It is hard to believe that this idyllic countryside was the centre of Britain's iron industry during the Middle Ages, but woods like those beside the line were the source of the charcoal upon which the industry depended.

A final climb through a cutting brings the train into the imposing four-platform station at Horsted Keynes. The size of the station – even equipped with a subway – is astonishing for so remote a location, but this was once the junction for a line to Haywards Heath that was still in use when the Bluebell began operations. The route of the line, which closed in 1963, can be seen going off behind the signal box on the left as you approach the station. Apart from the country park, ideal for picnics or for children to let off steam, Horsted Keynes has the Bluebell's carriage and wagon works and sheds, where the varied skills needed to maintain the stock are practised. It is also worth allowing time for a drink in the delightfully restored bar on the middle platform, which must have consoled many a weary traveller waiting for a connection.

Out of Horsted Keynes, another climb faces northbound trains as they approach Sharpthorne Tunnel, at 780yds (710m) the longest tunnel on any preserved railway. The pictures of Kingscote station following its purchase in 1985, before a team began work, are a good indication of what dedicated volunteers

can achieve. An entire platform had to be replaced, and the filled-in subway cleared out – quite apart from the eradication of both wet and dry rot in the station building.

Visitors to the Bluebell from the London area can take advantage of a ten-minute bus service that runs non-stop from East Grinstead station to Kingscote every day that the railway operates and coincides with the trains. Only visitors arriving at Kingscote by this bus are entitled to buy a ticket here, because of parking restrictions around the station. In a few years it should be possible to reach the Bluebell Railway by a simple cross-platform change at East Grinstead.

Isle of Wight Steam Railway
Isle of Wight
Smallbrook Junction, 1 mile (1.5km) south of Ryde

TRAIN SERVICE

MARCH TO MAY AND OCTOBER, THURSDAY AND SUNDAY; END MAY TO END SEPTEMBER, DAILY.

TEL: 01983 882204/884343

WEBSITE: WWW.IWSTEAMRAILWAY.CO.UK

Queen Victoria popularised the Isle of Wight by her regular visits to Osborne House and it was in Victorian times that the island became served by a characterful and extensive railway network, entirely worked by tank locomotives, and which carried huge numbers of holidaymakers.

The two lines that remain open could hardly be more different from each other, but they are linked by an interchange station, and the Ryde–Shanklin line, still part of the national railway system, is the best way to reach the Isle of Wight Steam Railway. First-time visitors from London to the island are often surprised by the train awaiting them as they step off the Wightlink ferry from Portsmouth at Ryde Pier – the last thing they would expect to see here is London Transport 1938 tube stock. Much of it was over 50 years old when it was brought across the Solent in 1989, so it conveys something of a museum feel to what is an excellent service. From Ryde it is a short journey by electric train to Smallbrook Junction where in 1991 Network SouthEast built a new station to serve the preserved steam railway. Anyone who recalls the days of steam on the island, would recognise most of the locomotives and carriages that run to Wootton, the western terminus of the 5-mile (8km) line.

RIGHT: TWO BRIGHTON 'TERRIERS', INCLUDING FORMER IWCR LOCOMOTIVE NO. 11, HAVE RETURNED HOME TO THE ISLE OF WIGHT.

RIGHT: THE IWSR's
OTHER RESTORED
'TERRIER', *FRESHWATER*.

BELOW: HAVENSTREET
STATION.

It is one of the particular pleasures of the Isle of Wight Steam Railway that almost all its carriages were built before World War I, and the standard of restoration is quite exceptional. Often passengers spend the first mile or two of a journey admiring the interior of their carriage, rather than

enjoying the scenery. The first part of the line, which takes you to the railway's headquarters at Havenstreet, is through woodland carpeted in bluebells in May, followed by views across fields to distant hills.

It is well worth stopping off at Havenstreet to look at the museum of the island's railways, found beside the shop in a former gasworks building. Rather surprisingly for a rural location, this structure was built as an act of benevolence by local landowner John Rylands, well-known to Mancunians for the library named after him. You can also visit engine shed under

supervision. The activity at Havenstreet today is in marked contrast to the peace of earlier times, when the tranquillity induced adders and a swan to find their way into the ground-level signal box – though not at the same time.

Kent & East Sussex Railway

Kent/East Sussex

Tenterden, 10 miles (16km) southwest of Ashford

TRAIN SERVICE

FROM MARCH TO OCTOBER. DAILY DURING AUGUST. SANTA SPECIALS AND THOMAS THE TANK ENGINE EVENTS.

TEL: 01580 765155

WEBSITE: WWW.KESR.ORG.UK

One of the most extraordinary characters in the history of British railways was Lt Col Holman Frederick Stephens. After studying civil engineering at London University, he went on to build some very marginal railways, providing links that the large railway companies had declined to construct. One of these was the Kent & East Sussex Railway, originally running from Robertsbridge to Headcorn via the Cinque Port of Tenterden. Another now preserved line with which he was involved as civil and mechanical engineer was the Ffestiniog Railway. None of his railways made more than slender profits and most lost money – a situation that was not allowed to continue for long after his death in 1931. The majority were gradually closed, but a goods service survived between Robertsbridge and Tenterden until 1961. A preservation bid was eventually successful after a court battle with the then Minister of Transport, and the first section re-opened in 1974. Today some 10.5 miles (17km) are operating between Tenterden and Bodiam, carrying passengers to the National Trust's magnificent 14th-century castle. There is still the possibility to extend the line the final 3 miles (5km) to Robertsbridge to link with the main Network Rail line.

Colonel Stephens' lines differed in character, but they had one thing in common – everything was done on a shoestring, including the engineering works and buildings, which were executed to the minimum standards or size possible. Many of the original buildings had been swept away by the time the preservationists took over, but several remained, most notably the station buildings at Tenterden where most passengers begin their journey. Indeed this was the only brick station building on the line – the others were of wood or corrugated iron. The adaptation of old buildings for the needs of visitors at Tenterden has been so well done that you would think the signal box had been opposite the station since the line opened in 1903; it was, in fact, rescued from Chilham between Ashford and Canterbury. The buffet is thought to be the oldest bus station in the country, possibly the oldest in the world; it was built in 1921 to serve Maidstone.

One of the pleasures of a journey on this line is its authentic collection of locomotives: one of the railway's two well-known 'Terrier' class locomotives actually worked on the railway during Colonel Stephens' years. Another diminutive tank engine, No 1556, was hired to the Kent & East Sussex during the 1930s and '40s. The railway's carriages are as heterogeneous a collection as might have been found on any of the Colonel's railways. Pride of place goes to the well-restored Victorian coaches, which range from rather spartan four-wheelers to a family saloon and the unique London & North Western Railway directors' saloon.

The 50-minute journey from Tenterden takes you steeply downhill through pasture and woods to Rolvenden, where the engine shed and workshops have been sited since Colonel Stephens' day. Here the tank locomotives and one tender engine are restored and maintained. Passing beside willow and reed-fringed channels on the right, the train skirts a former freshwater crayfish farm and heads out across flat fields that were once under the English Channel. The willows were planted during the 1930s in a rather sad gesture to augment the railway's meagre income.

The station at Wittersham Road may look all of a piece to anyone unversed in the nice distinctions of railway architecture, but the ensemble could hardly be more cosmopolitan. The station building came from north Wales, the water tower from Shrewsbury, the signals from Ireland and the signal box and lamps from Kent. The use of the word 'Road' was a kind of code that the railway companies used to indicate that the station was some distance from the village it purported to serve – in this case 3 miles (5km). However, the village with its windmill, oasthouse and even a Sir Edwin Lutyens' house, is well worth the walk.

The steep gradient that starts from the signal box at the platform end has the locomotive barking loudly through the cutting to the summit, after which a gentle curve leads on to the longest straight on the line as it crosses the Rother Levels to Northiam, with its beautifully restored station – a corrugated-iron original.

FAR LEFT: THE PULLMAN CAR *BARBARA* ONCE OPERATED ON MAIN LINE TRAINS FROM CHARING CROSS TO HASTINGS.

LEFT: THE EASY-GOING SPIRIT OF THE LIGHT RAILWAY IS APPARENT TO VISITORS.

Mid-Hants Railway

Hampshire

Alresford, 7 miles (11.5km) east of Winchester

Take the train from London Waterloo and you can be sitting on a Mid-Hants Railway train in little over an hour, simply by walking across the platform at Alton station. This easy interchange marked the culmination of more than ten years' hard work by the preservation society formed in 1973 to reopen what had been known locally as the Watercress Line. The objective was to save the 10 miles (16km) between Alton and the largely Georgian market town of Alresford.

The line opened originally in 1865, joining Alton and Winchester. It had an unremarkable life, except during the two world wars: in the first it was busy with traffic from Aldershot to Southampton Docks; and during the second the district around Alresford was briefly home to the 47th Infantry Regiment, 9th Division US Army. During the build-up to D-Day, newly built Winchester bypass became a tank park, and many tanks were unloaded at Alresford station.

The line saw occasional surges of traffic when it was used as a diversionary route while engineering work took place on the Waterloo–Southampton main line. For this purpose, the London & South Western Railway, which soon took over the independent company that built the line, had insisted it was built to main

RIGHT: STEAM LOCOMOTIVES NEED TO BE LUBRICATED FREQUENTLY.

BELOW: SR BULLEID BATTLE OF BRITAIN AT MEDSTEAD & FOUR MARKS STATION.

TRAIN SERVICE

WEEKENDS FROM JANUARY TO NOVEMBER AND SELECTED MID-WEEK DAYS FROM MAY TO SEPTEMBER. SANTA SPECIALS.

TEL: 01962 734866/733810

WEBSITE: WWW.WATERCRESSLINE.CO.UK

LEFT: THE MID-HANTS RAILWAY WAS AN ALTERNATIVE ROUTE FROM LONDON TO SOUTHAMPTON. RIGHT: A MAUNSELL MOGUL AS JAMES FROM THE *THOMAS THE TANK ENGINE* TALES.

line standards. This was to prove a great boon to the Mid-Hants Railway, for one of the problems encountered by some preserved railways is that a branch line ancestry usually prevents the use of heavy locomotives. To cope with the often unprecedented passenger figures, many short trains have to be run with small engines, or the railway has to upgrade structures to accept heavier locomotives.

Otherwise this line's claim to fame was the dispatch of watercress. The pure chalk-spring waters of the River Arle fostered this industry, which continues today. For almost a century the cress was packed into large wicker baskets, loaded at Alresford station into vans and sent up to London markets.

The railway survived a series of closure threats but finally succumbed in 1973. It was reopened between 1977 and 1985, the intention being to portray the character of a London & South Western/Southern Railway branch line. Each station is restored to represent a different era in the railway's history.

WARNING

STOP LOOK & LISTEN

BEFORE CROSSING THE LINE

Leaving from platform 3 at Alton, trains pass the newly positioned signal box and soon reach the site of Butts Junction where two other lines once led off, one to Fareham and the other to Basingstoke. (The latter achieved lasting fame through its use for the filming of two railway classics: *The Wrecker* in 1929 and *Oh! Mr Porter* in 1937.) The obvious exertions at the front end on this stretch are explained by the gradient of 1 in 60 up to the first station at Medstead & Four Marks; coupled with the almost equally steep descent from there to Alresford, drivers referred to taking trains 'over the Alps'.

To the south, soon after passing the site of Butts Junction, lies Chawton village where Jane Austen lived for eight years – her house is now a museum. The station buildings at Medstead & Four Marks are more modest than those at the other stations, simply because the stationmaster's house was built as a separate structure rather than incorporated in the platform building.

However, the most popular place to stop off is the other intermediate station, Ropley, for it is here that the Mid-Hants has its engine shed and workshops. There is also a picnic area, with playground facilities, providing a grandstand view of the shed yard and departures on the main line. Most obvious to passengers is the ornate topiary on the platform, which continues a tradition started many decades ago. As the train drops down to Alresford, you can see evidence of the watercress industry before the line enters a steep-sided chalk cutting on the approach to the southern terminus.

In 2004 the Mid-Hants was refurbishing Gresley, A4 Class No. 60019 *Bittern* which will hopefully be in steam by 2005.

LEFT: IT LOOKS LIKE A THOROUGHBRED, YET NO. 34016 *BODMIN* WAS RESCUED IN SCRAP CONDITION FROM WOODHAM BROS. YARD IN WALES AND RESTORED FOR SERVICE ON THE WATERCRESS LINE.

Romney, Hythe & Dymchurch Railway

Kent

Hythe, 4 miles (6.5km) south of Folkestone

Miniature railways have a fascination of their own, not least for children, witnessed by the enduring popularity of the Romney, Hythe & Dymchurch Railway since it opened in 1927. Although the number of miniature railways has mushroomed since World War II, the concept of the Romney, Hythe & Dymchurch remains unique. The reason for this is largely due to its creator, Captain Jack Howey, who had the wealth to build a main line railway in miniature, with double track, substantial stations and powerful locomotives capable of a scale speed of 75mph (120kph).

A strong commercial case for such lavishness would be hard to make – no miniature railway of comparable length has been able to justify more than a single line, for example. But with the rental income from a good chunk of central Melbourne in Australia, Captain Howey did not have to worry about sceptical bank managers. To power his trains, Howey ordered nine steam locomotives, five based on the elegant Pacific design by Sir Nigel Gresley for the London & North Eastern Railway, two freight types for aggregate traffic that never materialised and a pair of Canadian-style Pacifics – as you can imagine, Howey particularly enjoyed his railway holidays there.

The Duke of York, later King George VI, drove the first train into New Romney and the railway soon became well known as the World's Smallest Public Railway. It flourished during the 1930s and played its part in the defence of the Kent coast when an armoured train was built, sporting a couple of machine guns and an anti-tank rifle. Powered by a protected 4-8-2, *Hercules*, it made regular forays from its dummy hill near Dymchurch.

RIGHT: CROSSING THE EXPANSE OF THE SHINGLE
BANKS OF THE KENT COASTLINE, THE IMMACULATE
HENRY GREENLY 4-8-2 NO. 5 *HERCULES* POWERS
AN RH&DR TRAIN ON ITS WAY TO DUNGENESS.

Some economies were made on the railway as the popularity of holidays abroad eroded its traffic during the 1960s, but new management following Howey's death has helped to revive the railway's fortunes, and it remains one of the finest miniature railways in the world. Among many innovations is an observation car equipped with licensed bar. As well as being a tourist attraction, the Romney, Hythe & Dymchurch has a practical role in the community: since 1977 it has carried about 180 children a day from the Dymchurch area to and from school in New Romney.

Hythe is the largest resort on the line, with some fine Victorian hotels, and the terminal station still has the only original overall roof spanning its three platforms. It stands beside the Royal Military Canal, built to deter invasion by Napoleon. The station's size, coupled with the water tower, signal box, turntable and engine shed (now used to allow major refurbishment work) all help to create a main line atmosphere.

As the long train gathers pace under the signal gantry at the platform end, the line is fringed by back gardens on one

side and the remains of the canal on the other. The pace quickens as the line enters open country with wide views over the flat land of Romney Marsh, renowned for smuggling activities following the decline of the Cinque ports. In the distance can be seen the gently rising hills of Lympne, with its extraordinary castle built for Sir Philip Sassoon.

Bowling along the flat land towards Dymchurch at about 25mph (40kph), the clickety-clack of the rail joints provides a sound almost consigned to history on all but secondary routes on modern railways. After one of the line's many level crossings, the train reaches Dymchurch, which once had an overall roof, signal box and sidings. On the approach to the next station at St Mary's Bay, look out for the bungalow in which E. Nesbit spent the last years of her life, having achieved fame with *The Railway Children*; it is on the left as you enter the station and is named *The Long Boat*.

Open fields, a shallow cutting and a tunnel under a main road precede the railway's headquarters at New Romney. Apart from the attraction of watching engines coming off shed or shunting carriages, the station has a popular model

TRAIN SERVICE

DAILY FROM APRIL TO SEPTEMBER AND FEBRUARY AND OCTOBER HALF-TERMS; WEEKENDS IN MARCH AND FIRST HALF OF OCTOBER.

TEL: 01797 362353

WEBSITE: WWW.RHDR.ORG.UK

LEFT: MINIATURE LOCOMOTIVES FROM THREE CONTINENTS CROSS THE ROYAL MILITARY CANAL.

RIGHT: A ROMNEY PACIFIC, THE *GREEN GODDESS*.

BELOW: HENRY GREENLY ADAPTED HIS MINIATURE PACIFIC DESIGN INTO THE 'MOUNTAIN' CONFIGURATION FOR THE RH&DR.

exhibition with showcase models and two impressive model railways. Although the station has a huge new roof spanning the running lines, elements of Howey's original station survive, including the wooden clock tower.

Wartime damage to the line between New Romney and Dungeness wrecked the track so badly that the second line was never replaced. Now trains can cross at one point only, Romney Sands, on this section of the line that traverses one of the most unusual areas of Britain. For part of the way the line is fringed by bungalows at Greatstone, most of them built during the 1930s and many still retaining the architectural character of that decade.

The broad expanse of shingle that surrounds the two nuclear power stations and two lighthouses at Dungeness is for some an alien and barren landscape. But for anyone with an interest in natural history, it offers a diverse selection of rare plants with colonies of moths and butterflies, and is a sanctuary for birds. Having reached the end of the line, the 1904 lighthouse, with a rewarding panorama from the top, is a good reason to delay the return to New Romney.

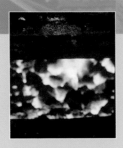

Want to be an Engine Driver?

There was a time when every boy wanted to be an engine driver when he grew up. For those who still harbour such atavistic ambitions, many preserved railways offer the chance to get your hands on the shovel and regulator. You can develop a sense of just what hard work it is to feed several tonnes of coal into a greedy firebox during a shift, or experience the thrill of the surge of power as the regulator is opened and steam rushes into the cylinders.

There are significant differences between the courses on offer around the country. Especially exciting are the ones available on the Great Central Railway which offers three levels of driver experience: Gold, Bronze and Silver. These all involve driving a full size locomotive on double track main line. They are unforgettable experiences which are popular as gifts. Gift vouchers are available from the Great Central.

All railways begin their courses with a preparatory talk about safety – the subject of paramount importance in all aspects of railway operations. This is usually followed by a talk about how steam locomotives work, the theory and practice of firing and the techniques of driving. On railways that have signal boxes, it is common for those on longer courses to have a session with a signalman to learn how to interpret fixed and hand signals. This condenses into hours what railwaymen took years to assimilate, so slow was progress through the grades from cleaner to top link driver.

Then comes the part that brings smiles to all – footplate experience. On longer courses, this will usually begin with pottering up and down outside the engine shed or in the goods yard. This is followed on railways (as opposed to centres), by a journey along the line; this can be a tall order for novices. Perhaps the most challenging is the 1 in 40 climb out of Bodmin Parkway on the Bodmin & Wenford Railway. Starting only yards from the end of the platform, this can tax the skill of experienced drivers on a wet day.

Some railways broaden the course further, such as that on the Gwili, which also includes the guard's duties and the full work of signalmen. However, for a weekend signalling course, you will need to go to the Severn Valley Railway, where an educational charity, the Kidderminster Railway Museum, organises such courses. Participants receive initial instruction in the museum, followed by visits to the signal boxes on the railway. Contact the Kidderminster Railway Museum, Comberton Hill, Kidderminster, Worcestershire. Alternatively, call 01562 825316 or visit the website www.krm.org.uk, for further information.

FAR LEFT: TWO YOUNGSTERS POSE WITH A BASSET-LOWKE MODEL OF *PRINCESS ELIZABETH* ALONGSIDE THE FULL-SIZE LMS PACIFIC.

LEFT: FOOTPLATE EXPERIENCE COURSES ARE NOW WIDELY AVAILABLE ON BRITAIN'S STEAM RAILWAYS.

RIGHT: THE SKILL OF THE FIREMAN IS A VITAL ELEMENT IN THE FOOTPLATE TEAM TO GET THE BEST PERFORMANCE OUT OF THE LOCOMOTIVE.

The Battlefield Line

Leicestershire

Shackerstone, 3 miles (5km) northwest of
Market Bosworth

TRAIN SERVICE

SATURDAYS, SUNDAYS AND BANK HOLIDAY MONDAYS,
FROM EASTER TO OCTOBER; ALSO DIESEL SERVICE
WEDNESDAYS, JULY AND AUGUST. SANTA SPECIALS.

TEL: 01827 880754

WEBSITE: WWW.BATTLEFIELD-LINE-RAILWAY.CO.UK

Bosworth Field is the battlefield in question, the place where, in 1485, Richard III was defeated and killed and Henry VII became the first Tudor king of England. The name given to the 4.5-mile (7km) line reflects the importance to the railway of that historic site, but the Battlefield Trail and Visitor Centre are not the only attractions for visitors to the railway.

Parallel to the approach road to Shackerstone station, where most passengers begin their journey, is the Ashby Canal on which barges began their trade in 1804. This, like the later railway which opened in 1873, was built to improve

 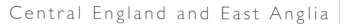

communications with the coalfield around Ashby and Moira. Leisure boats now use the canal, and the towpath makes for a pleasant walk as it keeps company with the railway to the south.

Schoolchildren make up a good proportion of the railway's passengers, since few educational resources can offer teachers the combination of a dynastic war and the age of steam. Shackerstone station museum displays an impressive if rather bewildering array of railway artefacts, including a telephone earpiece that tells railway tales, and visitors can soon understand the rudiments of signalling as well as pull levers. Every effort has been made to re-create the character of the country railway and demonstrate its importance to the community here, which witnessed the arrival of Edward VII in 1902 when he visited nearby Gopshal Hall (now demolished).

Only industrial locomotives are based permanently on the railway, but more powerful engines on loan from other railways or museums can often be seen at work. The gently undulating Leicestershire landscape rarely affords wide panoramas but the railway embankment gives something of a grandstand view as pheasants brazenly strut the neighbouring fields.

It is not currently possible to alight at Market Bosworth, the intermediate station, but the town is well worth exploring; it is extremely attractive, has a wonderful period feel and is the place where Samuel Johnson once taught at the grammar school. At journey's end the terminus beside the battlefield is served by the attractive station building from Leicester Humberstone Road, which was skilfully re-erected here. A path from the station leads to the trail around the battlefield, with information boards which take you back to that August day when the course of British history was decisively changed.

LEFT: A BUSY SCENE AT SHACKERSTONE STATION.
TOP: SHACKERSTONE HAS AN IMMENSE WEALTH OF RAILWAYANA AND SMALL EXHIBITS IN ITS CROWDED RAILWAY MUSEUM.

ABOVE: SHENTON STATION HAS BEEN RESTORED TO ITS ORIGINAL APPEARANCE.

Foxfield Steam Railway
Staffordshire
Blythe Bridge, 6 miles (9.5km) southeast of Stoke-on-Trent

A former colliery railway in the heart of the Staffordshire coalfield might seem to appeal to none but the most avid enthusiast, but don't be put off – the views from these trains are a far cry from bleak post-industrial landscapes. The spoil tips from the colliery are now largely overgrown, and for most of the journey the line passes through woods that threaten to engulf the train, so close are the branches, or past fields of grazing cows or corn. In the distance you can see the fringes of the Staffordshire moors, and across the valley is the village after which the line named its northern terminus, Dilhorne, recognisable by the octagonal spire of All Saints' church there.

Until the number of British coal mines was decimated, most collieries were connected to the railway system by sidings or by a branch line. Most of these have been built over or returned to nature, but close to Blythe Bridge station on the Stoke–Derby line is a surviving branch that served a mine in the once prosperous Staffordshire coalfield. Coal was mined at Foxfield in the 17th century, but it was 1893 before a branch was built off the North Staffordshire Railway, known locally as the 'Knotty' after the county emblem it adopted. The mine closed in

LEFT: THE HUNSLET AUSTERITY 0-6-0ST *WHISTON* PAUSES AT THE HEAD OF ITS TRAIN AT THE SUMMIT STATION ON THE FOXFIELD RAILWAY.

TRAIN SERVICE

FROM EASTER TO SEPTEMBER, SUNDAYS AND BANK HOLIDAY WEEKENDS. SANTA SPECIALS.

TEL: 01782 396210

WEBSITE: WWW.FOXFIELDRAILWAY.CO.UK

LEFT: THE RAILWAY WAS BUILT TO SERVE DILHORNE COLLIERY WHICH LIES AT THE FOOT OF A STEEP BANK, GUARANTEED TO TEST THE LINE'S INDUSTRIAL LOCOMOTIVES TO THE LIMIT.

NEXT PAGE: A PAIR OF SADDLETANKS GET TO GRIPS WITH A DEMONSTRATION COAL TRAIN AT THE FOOT OF THE GRADIENT OUT OF THE COAL YARD.

1965 but a 2.75-mile (4.5km) section was saved by a group of enthusiasts. More recently the railway has been awarded a Heritage Lottery Grant to enable it to go back to its roots. The grant will enable the purchase of the old mine, including the colliery headwinding frame, and aid their restoration. A new station and visitor centre will be created here. Within the centre, displays will cover the past history of the coal mine and the history of the Foxfield Steam Railway and how important it was for local industries.

To access this site, passengers will soon be able to experience the infamous Foxfield Bank which presently is only used for demonstrations. This will be a sight and sound not matched anywhere else, as the industrial locos climb the 1 in 19 gradient out of the old colliery which makes Foxfield so unique.

An engine shed and museum lie at the opposite end of the line close to Blythe Bridge. Visitors usually have a look round the collection of locomotives before taking a ride – all are tank engines and were once employed in industrial use, some of them in the Midland counties.

The small size of most of the Foxfield's locomotives means that the locomotives have to work hard pulling the former British Railways carriages. If you can, try to visit on one of the special days, when there is a demonstration of coal wagons being worked up the steep gradient from the colliery. These demonstrations provide a spectacle and sound that are unforgettable.

The railway has its own station bar, The One Legged Shunter, which serves a selection of real ales.

59

Great Central Railway
Leicestershire
Loughborough, 9 miles (14.5km) north
of Leicester

With so many preserved railways, it is difficult to offer something unique, but the Great Central Railway succeeds as the only line to re-create the atmosphere of the main line railway complete with double track and goods loops for expresses to overtake slower trains. The line is well placed to do this, since the route was once part of Britain's last great main line, the Great Central Railway, which ran from just north of Nottingham to a new London terminus at Marylebone. It was intended by its chairman, Sir Edward Watkin, to become part of a continuous railway from the north of England to France, through a tunnel under the English Channel which was to be built by an associated company. Today's Great Central serves as a reminder of that superbly engineered line, most of which was closed during the 1960s.

The starting point for most passengers is Loughborough, where the station is the largest in preservation. Film companies often take advantage of its size, emphasised by the long, ornate canopy along the island platform; the station was used for the filming of *Shadowlands*, starring Anthony Hopkins. Before boarding a train, passengers are invited to inspect the impressive workshops and engine shed, which can be reached by a footpath to the north of the station. The original signal box, that still controls train movements at the station, stands beside the path, and visitors are normally welcomed by the signalman. There is also a museum in part of the old lift shaft used for for luggage, which gives visitors a good idea of the history of the railway on which they are about to travel.

LEFT: A GCR FREIGHT LOCO MAKES AN ENERGETIC START WITH A HEAVY TRAIN IN WINTRY CONDITIONS OUTSIDE LOUGHBOROUGH CENTRAL.

RIGHT: WITH DOUBLE TRACK NOW RESTORED SOUTHWARDS FROM LOUGHBOROUGH, TODAY'S GCR RECAPTURES THE MAGIC OF A TRUE MAIN LINE.

As befits a main line railway, the Great Central has some large steam locomotives amongst its fleet and it frequently has visiting engines to add variety.

After leaving Loughborough for the half-hour journey, the first station, at Quorn & Woodhouse, has a picnic site adjacent to the typical island platform arrangement, in which tracks pass either side of a single platform. The station has been restored to its 1940s' wartime condition and every year, in June, hosts a huge wartime re-enactment event. Quorn & Woodhouse also boasts an award-winning signal box and fully operational period signalling. This was the winner of the Westinghouse Signalling Award at the National Railway Heritage Awards in 2003. Shortly beyond Quorn is the scenic highlight of the journey as the train crosses Swithland Reservoir on a long viaduct. Now a sanctuary for birds, the reservoir had to be drained for the construction

of the viaduct. It is at Swithland Sidings that the Great Central Railway's impressive work to restore the look of the old main line is best appreciated, though there is no station here. The goods loops have been installed and the whole section from Loughborough to Rothley is now fully operational with double track and signalling. You may also see a goods train of seemingly endless coal wagons pass by, for another Great Central project is the re-creation of the 'Windcutter' fast coal trains which once used the line. In order to achieve this, a large number of 16-ton mineral wagons has been assembled.

Try to break your journey at Rothley, for it is a delightful station with one of the best preserved rooms – the humble, but superbly refurbished parcels office. The station is gaslit and has been restored using the colours of the old Great Central Railway. The signal box was rescued from Wembley in London

TRAIN SERVICE

WEEKENDS ALL YEAR, ALL PUBLIC HOLIDAYS PLUS
WEEKDAYS FROM 2ND JUNE TO 20TH AUGUST AND
OTHER SELECTED WEEKDAYS, ALSO SANTA SPECIALS AT
CHRISTMAS.

TEL: 01509 230726

WEBSITE: WWW.GCRAILWAY.CO.UK

FAR LEFT: LMS STANIER PACIFIC NO. 46229
DUCHESS OF HAMILTON.

LEFT: LNER THOMPSON B1 CLASS 4 6 0 NO.
61264 AT LOUGHBOROUGH CENTRAL.

BELOW: SUNSET OVER SWITHLAND VIADUCT.

to replace the original, long since demolished. The large shed to the east of the line is the railway's carriage shed and works.

Just beyond the site of Belgrave & Birstall station, demolished in 1977, is the Great Central's new southern terminus. This promises to be one of the most ambitious ever projects in railway preservation, for the intention is to build a three-platform station with a two-storey building. A new engine shed, turntable and museum will be provided, with events, lawn and adjacent nature reserve.

One day the Great Central may run trains to the outskirts of Nottingham, because at the country park at Ruddington an affiliated group has created a northern base from which trains operate southwards for a couple of miles. Linking the two sections would double the present run of 7 miles (11.5km).

The Great Central operates throughout the year and the timetable includes non-passenger trains and demonstration freight trains as well as special runs by restored mail trains including picking up mail at speed – an incredible experience. There is also a non-stop express, *The Robin Hood*, which runs every Saturday and Sunday hauled by one of the six heritage main line diesel locomotives currently on the line.

Midland Railway – Butterley

Derbyshire

Ripley, 10 miles (16km) north of Derby

The Midland Railway Trust is not just for railway buffs, though it does have an excellent working line of 3.5 miles (5.5km) with three stations along the way. One of these stations also has a large museum, a farm park with lots of animals, a country park and a narrow gauge railway. Tourist railways are increasingly expanding their range of activities or points of interest to broaden their appeal and in this respect the Midland Railway – Butterley has succeeded admirably. The railway was something of a pioneer, starting off with a grandiose vision, and this was, in part, because it was the brainchild of local authorities who wanted to commemorate the railway which had had such an impact on the county town and its environs. Credit for the realisation of this bold plan, however, is due to the volunteer organisation formed to support the venture, since local government reorganisation ended the role of local authorities as the driving force.

The line itself is the remains of a Midland Railway branch that was built primarily for coal and goods traffic but also had a suburban service from Derby. At Hammersmith, the western terminus of the Centre, a line went off west to Ambergate. Its survival was largely due to the rail connection to the famous Butterley Company ironworks, set up in the 1790s. The ironworks' most famous contract was the roof for St Pancras station in London but it also exported widely, and ironwork for such stations as Buenos Aires was taken out by the Midland Railway for transfer to the docks.

RIGHT: FORMER SOMERSET & DORSET RAILWAY 2-8-0 NO. 53809 PASSES BENEATH AN ARRAY OF MR LOWER-QUADRANT SIGNALS WITH A DEMONSTRATION GOODS TRAIN.

A journey over this line begins at Butterley. There was nothing left of the original structures so the handsome station building was moved stone by stone from Whitwell in the north of the county. A model railway, buffet and shop help to pass the time before departure for Swanwick and Riddings Junction. The signal box at Butterley, one of four Midland Railway boxes on the line, was originally at the remote summit of Ais Gill on the Settle & Carlisle railway.

The museum (see below), best visited on the return from Riddings Junction, is passed on the right as the train steams past Swanwick Junction. As the valley opens up, you see cottages beside the Cromford Canal, and on a hillside to the south, a monument to William Jessop, who built the canal and helped to found the Butterley Company. At Riddings Junction the locomotive runs round the train before the return to Swanwick; in due course the line will be extended to a new station beside the Nottingham–Sheffield line.

The complex at Swanwick could take much of the day to see properly. It is dominated by the Matthew Kirtley Museum, named after a Midland locomotive superintendent who designed one of the locomotives on display. This huge building contains most of the railway's stock and also functions as a repair shop for both steam and diesel engines. Behind the shed is an engineering workshop, to which access is limited, and beyond that a miniature railway. A road transport museum is under construction for the display of a

TRAIN SERVICE

ON 214 DAYS DURING THE YEAR, WEDNESDAYS AND WEEKENDS.

TEL: 01773 570140

WEBSITE: WWW.MIDLANDRAILWAYCENTRE.CO.UK

LEFT: EARLY MORNING LOCOMOTIVE PREPARATION AT BUTTERLEY SHED.

collection ranging from early bicycles to double-decker buses. Past Johnson's Buffet (named after another Midland Railway locomotive superintendent) is Brittain Pit Farm Park, centred on a range of brick buildings, where you can see a wide variety of animals at close quarters. Near the demonstration signal box, where a signalman illustrates the intricacies of the job, a narrow gauge railway takes visitors into the 35-acre (14ha) country park. Here a network of paths leads to a series of ponds, to the remains of Grumblethorpe Colliery and to the mouth of the Cromford Canal tunnel. This was blocked off in 1909 following an earlier collapse through subsidence. The canal was finally abandoned in 1944, although recent restoration of the Ambergate–Cromford section has returned boats to that part of the waterway.

An alternative to taking the train back from Swanwick Junction is to walk along the top of the cutting between there and Butterley. However, westbound trains run through Butterley without stopping, so if you plan to do this, make sure you purchase a ticket for unlimited travel, which applies on all but a few special days. Then you can catch an outward train again, and return the whole way by rail.

The last section of the line is one of the most photographed, crossing a long stone embankment across Butterley Reservoir; this structure was built in the 1930s to replace a bridge. At Hammersmith, the locomotive again

runs round, under the control of a signal box rescued from Kilby Bridge, Leicester. Work is in progress here to create a small country station.

TOP RIGHT: WORKING IN ONE OF THE MOST HISTORIC SIGNAL BOXES IN ENGLAND, THE BUTTERLEY SIGNALMAN IS IN CHARGE OF THE FORMER AIS GILL BOX WHICH ONCE STOOD AT THE SUMMIT OF THE SETTLE & CARLISLE RAILWAY.

RIGHT: BUTTERLEY RESERVOIR

RIGHT: REPLICA OF TREVITHICK'S COALBROOKDALE LOCOMOTIVE AT THE COALBROOKDALE WORKS MUSEUM IN SHROPSHIRE.

Working Museums

BELOW: PART OF THE COLLECTION OF HISTORIC ROLLING STOCK OWNED BY THE BUCKINGHAMSHIRE RAILWAY CENTRE IS ON DISPLAY IN THE AIRY SURROUNDINGS OF THE FORMER LNWR REWLEY ROAD STATION FROM OXFORD WHICH WAS CAREFULLY RE-ERECTED AT QUAINTON ROAD.

Although visitors to the four principal operating museums would find them comparable, they each began in very different circumstances. The Great Western Society exists to preserve anything to do with that railway company – 'God's Wonderful Railway' as it has long been called, either with reverence or derision depending upon the speaker's allegiance. The Society's search for a home for its locomotives, carriages and wagons ended at the former Great Western Railway locomotive depot at Didcot in Oxfordshire. Here the Great Western Society has developed the museum to embrace signal boxes, signalling, historic railway buildings and small relics, displayed in a setting softened by trees and enlivened by two demonstration lines for operating days.

The Birmingham Railway Museum was founded not only as an engine shed for a growing collection of locomotives and carriages, but also as an engineering workshop to preserve the specialised machine tools developed to maintain the steam locomotive. With the end of steam on British Railways these were being discarded as rapidly as the locomotives themselves. Visitors can see something of the heavy engineering work in the workshop area. There is also a museum, a signal box to control the demonstration line and a turntable display area open Saturdays and Sundays.

At the Buckinghamshire Railway Centre you can stroll amongst the giants of the steam age on a 25-acre (10ha) site. The Centre boasts one of the largest private railway collections in Britain. Steam locomotives range from express passenger types to humble shunters. Numerous items of rolling stock include a coach from the Royal Train of 1901 and another used by Winston Churchill and General Eisenhower for wartime planning. Rides are available in vintage carriages and there is also an extensive miniature railway network. The Centre also includes Rewley Road Station built in 1851 and skilfully dismantled and moved in sections from the centre of Oxford.

Bressingham Steam Museum, at Diss in Norfolk, is largely the creation of Alan Bloom, a successful nurseryman with a passion for steam locomotives, and has no less than three different gauge railways.

The 15in (375mm) and 2ft (600mm) gauge lines take visitors around the nursery, while the standard gauge runs down an avenue of trees — modest tank engines would not look out of place here, but many visitors are astonished to see an engine the size of the Gresley, V2 Class 2-6-2 *Green Arrow* giving rides over a few hundred yards of track. There is also a magnificent display of traction engines, and many rare railway relics. Bressingham has the national collection of *Dad's Army* complete with a superb replica of Warmington on Sea. Quite apart from the joy of the railway and nurseries this alone is well worth a visit. Telephone 01379 686900 or visit the website www.bressingham.co.uk

LEFT: WIGAN COAL & IRON CO. BUILT VERY FEW STEAM LOCOMOTIVES, SO FOR ONE OF THEM TO SURVIVE INTO WORKING PRESERVATION IS A HAPPY ACCIDENT OF FATE. *LINDSAY*, BUILT IN 1887, IS IN THE STEAMTOWN RAILWAY MUSEUM.

ABOVE: BRESSINGHAM STEAM MUSEUM HAS TRACTION ENGINES AND AGRICULTURAL MACHINERY.

Nene Valley Railway

Cambridgeshire

Wansford, 8 miles (13km) west of Peterborough

The Nene Valley Railway has been a major asset to feature film-makers, since it is the only railway in Britain which has such an extensive overseas collection – locomotives and rolling stock from 11 different countries can be seen here. Well-known films whose foreign railway sequences were shot on the Nene Valley line include *Octopussy*, with Roger Moore as James Bond, *The Dirty Dozen* and *Murder on the Orient Express*.

This diverse collection was acquired partly by accident but also through necessity. By the time moves were afoot in the early 1970s to preserve a stretch of the railway along the Nene Valley, the only available locomotives in Britain were those languishing in Barry scrapyard in south Wales.

Exposure to salt air over many years made them costly to restore. Moreover, Peterborough Development Corporation, which had bought the line from British Rail, wanted to see trains running quickly. An offer of a Swedish engine seemed to be the answer to the problem, not least because it was necessary to demolish only one overbridge to make the line useable by locomotives built to the larger continental loading gauge. The Nene Valley soon attracted other foreign engines, and visitors can see examples from

TRAIN SERVICE

SUNDAYS FROM JANUARY TO MARCH, WEEKENDS FROM APRIL TO OCTOBER, AND A VARIABLE MIDWEEK SERVICE FROM JUNE TO AUGUST. SANTA SPECIALS.

TEL: 01780 784444

WEBSITE: WWW.NVR.ORG.UK

France, Germany, Austria, Poland, Sweden and Denmark. The railway also has a good collection of British engines, if the propensity to stick all the plumbing outside the boiler is not to your taste.

This line is very good for children. It has a locomotive permanently called *Thomas*, named by the Reverend W. Awdry himself, and young visitors particularly relish the tunnel. There is also the 2,000-acre (808ha) Nene Park – an ideal place to break the journey, and served by the intermediate station at Ferry Meadows – which has play areas for children, a miniature railway, cycle hire, nature trails and picnic sites.

ABOVE: CROSSING THE TRESTLE VIADUCT OVER THE RIVER NENE.
LEFT: ALMOST 10,000 GERMAN-DESIGNED KRIEGSLOK 2-10-0 HEAVY FREIGHT ENGINES WERE BUILT IN WORLD WAR II.

RIGHT: THE SWEDISH B CLASS 4-6-0 HAS BEEN REPAINTED IN AN ATTRACTIVE BLUE LIVERY, WHICH SUITS ITS RAKISH LINES VERY WELL. LIKE ALL SWEDISH STEAM LOCOS, IT IS WELL PROVIDED WITH ELECTRIC LIGHTS ALL ROUND.

LEFT: THE RIVER NENE AND ITS WATER MEADOWS ARE NEVER FAR FROM THE RAILWAY.

Most passengers start their journey at the line's headquarters at Wansford, where you can also look round the engine shed. The original station building – an architectural gem in Jacobean style by the accomplished architect William Livock – is sadly not owned by the Nene Valley Railway, although their signal box is one of the finest on a preserved railway. Trains head west through the 671-yard (614m) Wansford Tunnel to the site of Yarwell Junction, where lines to Rugby and Northampton divided. Here trains reverse and head back through Wansford, cross the river and turn into the 3-mile (5km) straight to Ferry Meadows. Passing broad cornfields, followed by the man-made country park, the line terminates at Orton Mere in Peterborough, a short walk from the main line station.

North Norfolk Railway
The Poppy Line
Sheringham, 4 miles (6.5km) west of Cromer

The 25-minute journey on the North Norfolk Railway might be an eye-opener for those who think of Norfolk as a flat county. For much of the outward journey over the 6 miles (9.5 km) from Sheringham to Holt, the locomotive has to work hard on gradients as steep as 1 in 80, but the open embankments enable passengers to enjoy the marvellous views over the sea to the north and the woods inland.

Once part of the Midland & Great Northern Railway, the section that forms today's North Norfolk Railway was built to cater as much for holiday traffic as to serve local communities, but the seasonal nature of the line's income led to its downfall. It closed in stages between 1959 and 1964, although a new station at Sheringham can still be reached by train from Norwich and it is only a few minutes' walk between the stations.

Reopened to passengers in 1975, the original Sheringham station reflects the number of passengers it handled when named trains like *The Broadsman* and *Norfolkman* called here. The elaborate cast-iron brackets supporting the canopy are adorned with hanging baskets, and there is plenty to look at while waiting for the next train, including artefacts illustrating the history of the Midland & Great Northern Railway.

After viewing the delightful landscape on the way to Weybourne, passengers will not be surprised to learn that it has been designated an Area of Outstanding

LEFT: TWO GREAT EASTERN LOCOMOTIVE DESIGNS SIDE-BY-SIDE AT SHERINGHAM.

ABOVE: TIME FOR THE DRIVER TO RELAX.

TRAIN SERVICE (STEAM AND HERITAGE DIESEL)

DAILY FROM APRIL TO SEPTEMBER AND MOST DAYS IN OCTOBER; WEEKENDS IN MARCH AND NOVEMBER. MANY SPECIAL EVENTS THROUGH THE YEAR.

TEL: 01263 820800
TALKING TIMETABLE: 01263 820808

WEBSITE: WWW.NNR.CO.UK

RIGHT: THE HUNSLET 0-6-0ST *RING HAW* BRINGS ITS TRAIN ROUND THE CURVE INTO WEYBOURNE WITH THE NORTH SEA IN THE DISTANCE.

BELOW: *RING HAW* PAUSES AT WEYBOURNE.

ABOVE: A RUNNING NUMBER, BTC REGISTRATION PLATE AND BUILDER'S PLATE FROM A DIESEL LOCO.

Natural Beauty. Once a golf course on the seaward side is left behind, the land on either side is attractive arable country with fields of barley, carrots and sugar beet. Inland the fields rise up to the woodlands of Sheringham Park, by Humphry Repton, and regarded by him as his finest work. It is also interesting to see the railway from the park – a viewpoint which puts the trains into the perspective of a fine panorama of coastline and agricultural hinterland.

The intermediate station at Weybourne offers several reasons to postpone the final leg of the journey to Holt. It is here that locomotives are restored, and guided tours may be possible. Call 01263 820800 to enquire. A board on the station suggests walks through nearby Kelling Woods, and in the opposite direction, a mile from the station, is the village of Weybourne. As well as the ruins of an Augustinian priory and windmill, walkers are close to Weybourne Hope where exceptionally deep water made it a likely place for an attempted invasion in 1588 and again during World War II. The section to

Holt climbs across Kelling Heath with good views out to sea. At Holt Station, the original M&GN station from Stalham has been re-erected. In high season, passengers are often met by a horse-bus for conveyance into the Georgian market town.

TRAIN SERVICE

DAILY FROM APRIL TO SEPTEMBER, THOUGH NO MONDAY OR FRIDAY SERVICE EXCEPT BANK HOLIDAYS AND IN JULY AND AUGUST. SANTA SPECIALS.

TEL: 01678 540666

WEBSITE: WWW.BALA-LAKE-RAILWAY.CO.UK

Bala Lake Railway

Gwynedd

Llanuwchllyn, 13 miles (21km) north of Dolgellau

There is something special about railways that run alongside an expanse of water, and no tourist railway can rival the 1ft 11⅝in (600mm) gauge Bala Lake Railway, for it is seldom out of sight of its accompanying acres of water. Beyond are the peaks of the Aran Mountains, some rising to almost 3,000ft (914m).

Most visitors begin their 25-minute journey at the southern terminus of Llanuwchllyn, because the temporary terminus outside Bala has limited facilities and access. A ¾-mile (1.2km) extension to a new station closer to the centre was planned but planning problems have prevented its construction. The station at Llanuwchllyn was once a crossing place on the single line standard gauge railway that linked the coast at Morfa Mawddach, beyond Dolgellau, with Corwen and Ruabon. This was closed by Dr Beeching in 1965, along with hundreds of miles of other Welsh railways.

Re-opened in stages from 1972, the Bala Lake Railway now runs for 4.5 miles (7km) and is the best way to enjoy the scenery around the lake – the parallel road requires total concentration from car drivers. Before boarding the train, it is worth having a look in the 1896 signal box, which still controls the points and signals and is often open to passengers. Trains are normally hauled by one of the three steam locomotives. Appropriately, two of them once worked in the Dinorwic slate quarries at Llanberis. As the railway joins the lake, a large house can be seen across the water: Glanllyn Hall was the Williams Wynne family home and is now an outdoor activities centre. Sir Watkin Williams Wynne

ABOVE: *MAID MARIAN* IS A HUNSLET 0-4-0ST WHICH WAS BUILT FOR SERVICE IN DINORWIC SLATE QUARRY IN 1903.

LEFT: THE RAILWAY'S ARMORIAL DEVICE AS DISPLAYED ON ITS COACHING STOCK.

was a shareholder of the company that built the line, and when he disembarked at Glanllyn Halt a flag would be hoisted to summon his boat.

The line meanders beside the lake, the occasional headland seeming to take the railway inland. Anglers are often seen, some doubtless attracted by the lake's unique primitive species of fish, the gwyniad, which has been protected since 1988. A variety of walks from Llangower station entice some passengers to break their journey, while the historic market town of Bala is only ten minutes' walk from the terminus.

ABOVE: MAID MARIAN'S WORKSPLATE PROCLAIMING HER DATE AND BUILDER. THIS IS EFFECTIVELY A LOCOMOTIVE'S BIRTH CERTIFICATE.

LEFT: QUARRY HUNSLETS HAVE PROVED THEMSELVES IDEAL SMALL LOCOMOTIVES FOR PASSENGER WORK ON NARROW GUAGE TOURIST LINES. THERE ARE ATTRACTIVE LAKESIDE VIEWS ALONG ALMOST ALL OF THE BLR.

Brecon Mountain Railway
Powys
Pant, 2 miles (3km) north of Merthyr Tydfil

The impressive railway headquarters are situated at Pant, to the north of Merthyr Tydfil, in an area that was an early cradle of industrial invention and enterprise. The legacy of this activity can still be seen during a journey on the Brecon Mountain Railway, which is largely built on the trackbed of the standard gauge line that once linked Merthyr Tydfil to Brecon. A ramp takes visitors up from the car park and booking office to platform level, where, from a gallery, you can view the well-equipped workshops and repair work on locomotives.

The most used locomotive is the beautifully kept maroon *Graf Schwerin-Löwitz*, built in 1908 for a narrow gauge railway in eastern Germany. It usually

Narrow gauge railways never found favour in Britain on the scale that they did in most other countries throughout the world. Only in north Wales was there a significant mileage. So it is not surprising that new narrow gauge tourist railways have had to look abroad for their motive power. The 1ft 11¾inch (600mm) Brecon Mountain Railway is a good example: of its four steam locomotives, only one worked in Britain, are from South Africa and one from the former East Germany.

hauls four observation coaches and a caboose based on a design for a narrow gauge railway in Maine, USA; this vehicle is ideal for visitors in wheelchairs. As the train pulls out, the remains of adjacent quarries to the west indicate the source of limestone for the ironworks which made Merthyr Tydfil famous.

Evidence of quarrying can be seen throughout the 3-mile (5km) journey to Dol-y-Gaer, but it does not detract from the grandeur of the scenery as the railway enters the Brecon Beacons National Park. Streams tumble down the wooded

RIGHT: THE GRAND SCENERY OF THE BRECON BEACONS NATIONAL PARK AND TAF FECHAN RESERVOIR.

hillsides, some feeding the Taf Fechan reservoir, behind which three peaks of the Brecon Beacons rise up. The middle peak, Pen-y-Fan, is the highest in south Wales at 2,907ft (886m). The reservoir holds 3,400 million gallons and was built in 1927.

From Pontsticill there are attractive walks along the edge of the reservoir.

Ffestiniog Railway

Gwynedd

Porthmadog, 18 miles (29km) south of Caernarfon

TRAIN SERVICE

DAILY FROM LATE MARCH TO EARLY NOVEMBER; WEEKENDS IN LATE FEBRUARY/MARCH. SANTA SPECIALS.

TEL: 01766 516000

WEBSITE: WWW.FESTRAIL.CO.UK

The history of the Ffestiniog Railway is reassuring evidence that events in the remotest of places can make a significant impact on world history. Testimony to this was given by no less a personage than the Russian Tsar, who sent the Ffestiniog's manager and engineer a gold medallion and silver shield in recognition of the railway's influence. The interest of Victorian railway engineers and builders in the Ffestiniog Railway was due to its narrow gauge of 1ft 11½ inch (600mm) and its pioneering use of steam locomotives. But the railway would never have come into being at all had not William Maddocks, local landowner and Member of Parliament for Boston in Lincolnshire, built the great embankment called the Cob across the estuary of Traeth Mawr, which was opened in 1811. This

diverted water channels and led to the scouring of the natural harbour that became the slate transhipment dock of Port Madoc, now Porthmadog. A 13.5-mile (20km) railway was built to link Port Madoc with the slate quarries at Blaenau Ffestiniog. The Ffestiniog Railway opened in 1836 using gravity for the descent from Blaenau and horses to pull the empty wagons back up the hill. The horses recovered their strength while riding downhill in 'dandy' wagons. The growth in demand for slate, spurred by the Industrial Revolution and the growth of towns and cities, necessitated the adoption of steam for haulage. The Ffestiniog's manager, Charles Spooner, commissioned the London engineers George England & Co. to design and build four small locomotives, the first for commercial use on such a small gauge. Two arrived in 1863 and the other two the following year. Passengers were first carried officially in 1865, their custom becoming ever more important to the railway as tourism flourished and slate carrying declined.

It was the next great innovation that was to attract the Tsar's emissary, Count Bobrinsky. In 1870 trials were held with a recently delivered double bogie steam locomotive designed by James Fairlie – its articulation permitted a long boiler with central firebox, and Fairlie's name was given to the type. Shortly afterwards the Ffestiniog Railway became not only the first narrow gauge railway to try bogie passenger coaches but one of the first railways in Britain to employ them. Descendants of the double fairlie type still take the Ffestiniog Railway's passengers from sea level up to 710 feet (216m).

LEFT: A FFESTINIOG DOUBLE-FAIRLIE BLACKS OUT THE DAYLIGHT STARTING FROM PORTHMADOG HARBOUR STATION. RIGHT: FORGING A ROUTE THROUGH MOUNTAINOUS COUNTRY REQUIRED MASTERLY CIVIL ENGINEERING.

Harbour station, on the southeastern edge of Porthmadog, contains an excellent café and bar so that passengers can relax between their journeys. Crossing the Cob as the train leaves Porthmadog, you see a panorama of mountains including, to the northeast on a clear day, Mount Snowdon. On the opposite side, waves lap the massive rocks that strengthen Maddocks' work. As the line swings round through 90 degrees at the end of the Cob, the Ffestiniog's works and carriage and engine sheds can be seen to the right. They were named Boston Lodge after Maddocks' Lincolnshire constituency.

The climb begins here and barely lets up all the way to Blaenau. At the first station, Minffordd, the site of interchange sidings with the main line that runs along the coast can be seen to the left. Passengers can still conveniently change trains here. Beyond the single platform at Penrhyn the line enters the Snowdonia National Park. From here on the scenery is seldom less than spectacular, the line often twisting along the contours of the hills with long drops to the valley floor.

As the line approaches the isolated crossing station at Tan-y-Bwlch, a descending train can often be seen nearing the station on the opposite side of the valley. It was here during the 1930s and 1950s that the station mistress, Bessie Jones, attired in Welsh costume, dispensed home-made teas. A number of walks can be taken from Tan-y-Bwlch station, for which the operators

ABOVE: HUNSLET SADDLETANKS *LINDA* AND *BLANCHE* FROM THE PENRHYN QUARRY WORKING DOUBLE-HEADED ON THE ASCENT TO BLAENAU FFESTINIOG.

thoughtfully provide a leaflet, *Where to go and what to do from Ffestiniog Railway stations*.

Dduallt station marks the beginning of the Deviation, forced on the railway by the submersion of the old trackbed by the lower reservoir of the pumped storage scheme near Tanygrisiau.

Construction began in 1965 and people from all walks of life, many with no interest in railways, volunteered to help to build the new railway. It was no simple task, entailing construction of the only spiral on a public railway in Britain and a new Moelwyn Tunnel.

The old trackbed and tunnel mouth can be seen as the train climbs away from the loop and plunges into the 287-yard (262m) tunnel. The train emerges to skirt Tanygrisiau Reservoir and squeeze past the backs of houses into Blaenau, the hills a jumble of slate and rock from two centuries of extraction. Journey's end is a new interchange station opened with the help of British Rail and the county council, enabling passengers to reach the Ffestiniog Railway from the north Wales coast at Llandudno Junction.

Gwili Railway
Dyfed
3 miles (5km) north of Carmarthen

TRAIN SERVICE

THE RAILWAY RUNS FROM APRIL TO OCTOBER AND DECEMBER. IT IS OPEN EVERY DAY DURING SCHOOL AND HALF TERM HOLIDAYS, AT OTHER TIMES ON SUNDAY AND WEDNESDAY. SANTA SPECIALS – DECEMBER AND 'DAY OUT WITH *THOMAS*' EVENTS – EASTER AND OCTOBER HALF TERM.

TEL: **01267 230666**

WEBSITE: WWW.GWILI-RAILWAY.CO.UK

BELOW: VOLUNTEERS HAVE WORKED HARD TO RE-CREATE ALL OF THE FACETS OF THE GWILI RAILWAY FROM SCRATCH.

At present the Gwili Railway is only 2 miles (3km) long, running from Bronwydd Arms to Danycoed, but what it lacks in length it makes up for in scenery and the high standards it has set itself for the future. In 2001 the line was extended to a new station in Danycoed. The company has a major development plan to extend the line southwards to Carmarthen which will be its new terminal. The Gwili Railway already owns the trackbed to the Carmarthen by-pass at Abergwili. As its name suggests, the line follows the River Gwili along a gently sloped valley, passing well wooded hillsides and meadows on its way to Danycoed. At Llwyfan Cerrig, where there is no road access, you'll find a riverside picnic site and miniature railway.

The basis of the railway is the long cross-country line once operated by the Great Western Railway between Aberystwyth and Carmarthen. This line served Derry Ormond, Strata Florida and Caradog Falls Halt, taking three hours to cover 60 miles (96.5km) due to the number of stations and the single track line. In the 1920s, passengers at Aberystwyth could enjoy a *thé dansant* on a sprung dance floor provided by GWR in its new station building.

Passenger services ended in 1965 and the last freight was carried on the southern section in 1973, but the Gwili Railway stepped in to create the first standard gauge preserved railway in Wales. Everything you see has been done by volunteers – tracklaying, dismantling and re-erecting railway buildings, as well as the restoration of carriages and locomotives. Help has arrived from various sources. Railway enthusiasts from Brynteg School, for example, have restored an 1891 Taff Vale Railway coach that served for half a century as a farmer's shed following its withdrawal from service in 1926. Examine the flower-decorated signal box at Bronwydd Arms which has been so well transposed from its original home at Llandybie on the Central Wales line that you would think it had always been there.

Llanberis Lake Railway

Gwynedd

Llanberis, 6 miles (9.5km) east
of Caernarfon

Slate was the original reason for the existence of most of today's tourist railways in north Wales, and a journey on the Llanberis Lake Railway can be combined with a visit to the adjacent Welsh Slate Museum, offering a marvellous insight into the industry's history. Both are near the village of Llanberis, once home to many of the 3,000 workmen employed at the nearby Dinorwic Quarries and also the start of the Snowdon Mountain Railway.

The Llanberis Lake Railway uses part of the trackbed of the former Padarn Railway, built to join the quarries to the harbour at Port Dinorwic, and the museum occupies the imposing slate building that formed the quarry and railway workshops. Besides a visit to the museum, it is worth allowing time to follow the trails around the spectacular Vivian Quarry, in which sheer walls of slate rise up from the flooded centre, and to look round the visitor centre in the former quarry hospital.

Trains are hauled by one of three 1ft 10¾ inch (600mm) gauge steam locomotives that once hauled slate wagons around the upper galleries at Dinorwic Quarries to the head of the inclined planes. The wagons were then lowered down to the larger 4ft (1,200mm) Padarn Railway on which they were carried piggyback to waiting ships.

Starting from Gilfach Ddu station, beside the car park shared with the Slate Museum, Llanberis Lake Railway trains begin their journey with a ride on the newly opened extension up to Llanberis village, passing historic Dolbadarn Castle on the way. Passengers can break their journey here if they wish, as the new station is convenient for a combined visit to Snowdon Mountain Railway, as well as the shops, hotels and restaurants of Llanberis High Street. From here the train runs non-stop to the other end of the line at Penllyn. After retracing the route back to Gilfach Ddu, the line enters a cutting through slate tips, leading to an impressive arch dated 1900. Beyond here the scenery opens out, and for the rest of the 60-minute return trip the line

LEFT: PASSENGER TRAINS NOW RUN BY LLYN PADARN, WHERE ONCE SLATE WAS CARRIED.

TRAIN SERVICE

DAILY FOM APRIL TO SEPTEMBER, AND ON SELECTED DAYS IN MARCH AND OCTOBER.

TEL: 01286 870549

WEBSITE: WWW.LAKE-RAILWAY.CO.UK

is seldom more than a few feet from the edge of Lake Padarn. The carriages allow almost unobstructed views across the water to the village of Llanberis and the slopes of Snowdon, on which you can sometimes see a plume of steam as a Snowdon Mountain Railway train crawls slowly up the mountain.

On arrival at the terminus at Penllyn the locomotive uncouples and runs round the train, whilst the guard takes the opportunity to check tickets. Although you can leave the train here, it is not recommended as there is no road access and only a rough footpath links the station with the outside world. On the homeward run the train makes a short stop halfway down the lake at Cei Llydan, where you can break your journey and return on a later train. Here there are picnic tables, benches beside the lake, and an adventure playground and woodland centre in the trees on the opposite side of the line.

LEFT: THIS PICTURESQUE LINE HAS THREE OF THE FORMER DINORWIC QUARRY HUNSLET SADDLETANKS, *ELIDIR*, *WILD ASTER* AND *DOLBADARN*.
BELOW: THE REMARKABLE 1848 PADARN RAILWAY LOCOMOTIVE, *FIRE QUEEN*, WHICH YOU CAN SEE AT PENRHYN CASTLE MUSEUM.

Llangollen Railway
Denbighshire
Llangollen, 11 miles (18km) north of Oswestry

BELOW: GWR PRAIRIE TANK NO. 4141 IN THE DEE VALLEY.

RIGHT: LLANGOLLEN STATION IS IN THE HEART OF TOWN, OVERLOOKING THE RIVER DEE.

The 7-mile (11.5km) Llangollen Railway is hard to beat for the glorious Welsh landscape it passes through on the half-hour journey between Llangollen and Carrog. Before closure to passengers by British Railways in 1965, the line was used by excursion trains and today, in preservation, the Llangollen Railway still provides access to the scenic delights of the Dee Valley that motorists would otherwise miss.

The railway lay derelict for nearly a decade after the track was lifted, but in 1975 a group of preservationists received the keys to Llangollen Station and began the task of rebuilding the

TRAIN SERVICE

DAILY FROM THE BEGINNING OF APRIL TO THE BEGINNING OF OCTOBER. REFER TO TIMETABLE FOR OTHER MONTHS. SANTA SPECIALS IN DECEMBER.

TEL: 01978 860979
TALKING TIMETABLE: 01978 860951

WEBSITE: WWW.LLANGOLLEN-RAILWAY.CO.UK

BELOW: GREAT WESTERN AND LMS MOTIVE POWER IN DOUBLE-HARNESS AT LLANGOLLEN STATION.

line westward towards Corwen, some 10 miles (16km) distant. By 1996 the present western terminus of Carrog had been reached and a period of consolidation began.

Viewed from Llangollen Bridge, the station stands beside the River Dee with the hills providing a superb backdrop to Eisteddfod town. Dominating the skyline to the north are the ruins of Castell Dinas Bran, whilst to the southwest is Plas Newydd, famous as the home of the Ladies of Llangollen.

The steam locomotive fleet is predominantly of Great Western origin, including No.7822 *Foxcote Manor* that once hauled the Royal Train, plus others appropriate to North Wales. There are also a number of industrial steam and diesel locomotives based on the line.

As the train leaves Llangollen it climbs through a cutting with the locomotive shed and workshops on the right at a higher level in the former goods yard. Before the railway closed, up to

four daily goods trains called there but today it is where the Llangollen Railway restores and maintains its locomotives. As you approach Goods Junction, the connection from the yard appears on the right and that line continues towards Pentrefelin Carriage and Wagon Depot with the Llangollen Canal visible behind it. The train curves away past Pentyrefelin Depot, crosses the Dee Bridge with fine views of the river and climbs up the gorge to Berwyn Station. The mock Tudor-style station has a small tearoom where, on busy weekends, refreshments

are served. The building was designed to match the Chain Bridge Hotel on the opposite bank of the river. The hotel takes its name from the adjacent suspension footbridge which has been out of use, although there are hopes it will be restored.

Departing from Berwyn the train crosses the six-span Berwyn Viaduct, the renovation of which earned the Llangollen Railway Trust a prestigious award at the Historic Bridge and Infrastructure Awards in London in 2003. There is then a spectacular vista to the right of the surrounding countryside including Llantisilio Hall and the Horseshoe Falls designed by Thomas Telford, from which the Llangollen Canal receives its water supply. Shortly afterwards the train threads the murky darkness of Berwyn Tunnel (689 yards/630m) before emerging into a wooded area as it approaches the remote Deeside Halt.

LEFT: WITH VISITING GWR GOODS ENGINE NO. 3205 TO THE FORE, THE DOUBLE-HEADED CAMBRIAN COAST EXPRESS STORMS UP THE VALLEY FROM LLANGOLLEN.

ABOVE: DAVID SHEPHERD'S 9F 2-10-0 NO. 92203 BLACK PRINCE.

Deeside was the site of a passing loop opened in 1908 to split the length of the single line section between Llangollen and Glyndyfrdwy. A new signal box has replaced the original demolished when the line closed, and the platform and building have only existed in the preservation era. The Halt is popular with walkers but passengers must remember to advise the guard if they wish to disembark because trains only stop on request. Anyone waiting to catch a train must give a clear hand signal to the driver, like hailing a bus.

Beyond Deeside, the valley opens out as it approaches the station at Glyndyfrdwy with its level crossing and loop where trains pass each other. If the station looks familiar, you may have seen it on television when it featured in an *Eastenders* special called *Dot's Story*. The tearoom is open at busy times.

From Glyndyfrdwy to Carrog you are travelling over the section of railway where the Railhill Trails of 1829 were restaged in 2002 by the BBC *Timewatch* programme using three replica locomotives, *Rocket*, *Sans Pariel* and *Novelty*. Once again *Rocket* won but it was a close run thing! The line is now relatively straight for some distance, with the valley widening out, before curving past Glyndwr's Mount. Owain Glyndwr was born in Glyndyfrdwy in the 14th century and the mount is said to have been the site of his summer palace.

Carrog Station has been superbly restored. It is difficult to believe only the main station building is original and the signal box and waiting room have had to be rebuilt using mainly salvaged materials. The tearoom is a popular destination for those arriving at the station. For those favouring a little light exercise, Carrog and the River Dee are just a short stroll away. Beyond Carrog Station, the track continues tantalisingly in the direction of Corwen for a short distance where an engineers' siding has been provided in readiness for a further expansion.

Severn Valley Railway
Worcestershire/Shropshire
Kidderminster, 5.5 miles (9km) south of Stourbridge

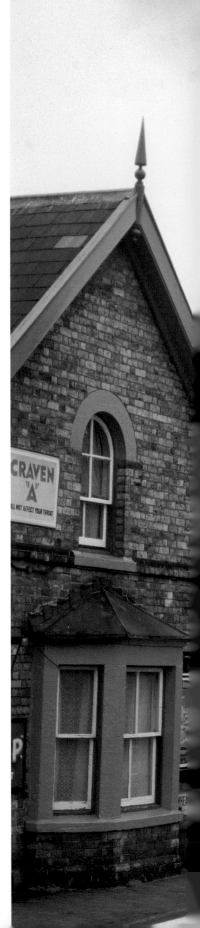

The Severn Valley Railway has reason enough for its claim to be Britain's premier steam railway. At 16 miles (25km), it is one of the longest lines; it passes through some of the most delightful scenery to be enjoyed on a tourist railway; the service is busy enough at peak periods to require five trains in operation; its stations are superbly restored and quite individual in character; and it has one of the most varied collections of locomotives and rolling stock. Yet the character of a 70-minute journey over the line can vary enormously. In common with other railways that operate a service for most of the year, the atmosphere fluctuates from that of a busy cross-country railway, with powerful tender engines pulling long trains during the high season, to a quiet country branch line off season.

Try a weekend in mid-March or even November, when the short trains are usually hauled by tank engines, and stay until the last train of the day. At Highley, one of the smaller intermediate stations, only a handful of passengers await the train, the gas lamps cast an unfamiliar glow over the platform, and the only sounds are of birds in the wooded hillside above the station. The ring of bells in the signal box, the rustle of signal wires and the metallic drop of lever locks herald the arrival of your train. Its headlamps glowing, the engine rounds the curve with the orange glare from the firebox illuminating the driver and fireman. The cold air produces clouds of steam as the small-wheeled tank briskly climbs away to Bridgnorth. Such experiences are the essence of preserved railways.

For almost 20 years, from the arrival of the first locomotive and four carriages in 1967, the historic Shropshire town of

ABOVE: VOLUNTEER FOOTPLATEMEN RELAXING AT BRIDGNORTH.

RIGHT: A PAIR OF GREAT WESTERN LOCOMOTIVES CHARGE THROUGH ARLEY STATION.

TRAIN SERVICE

EVERY WEEKEND AND DAILY FROM EARLY MAY TO LATE SEPTEMBER PLUS FEBRUARY, APRIL AND OCTOBER SCHOOL HOLIDAYS. SANTA SPECIALS.

TEL: 01299 403816/0800 600 900

WEBSITE: WWW.SVR.CO.UK

Bridgnorth was the headquarters of the Severn Valley Railway. The line was progressively reopened to the south until 1984 when the final section, from Bewdley to Kidderminster, reconnected the railway to, what was then, the British Rail network. By redeveloping the goods yard at the Worcestershire carpet town, the Severn Valley was able to build an imposing new terminus in traditional Great Western Railway style.

Kidderminster then became the railway's main station, the short walk between the stations encouraging passengers to use the frequent trains from Birmingham. A connection with the Birmingham–Worcester line also enables through excursions on to the Severn Valley Railway. Before boarding a train, it is worth spending time in Kidderminster Railway Museum, which provides an introduction to all the paraphernalia that railway companies produced as part of their operations – from signal-box lever frames, which visitors can work, to the lunch boxes of footplate crews.

As departing trains negotiate the points at the station throat, they pass the signal box on the left and the railway's turntable

and carriage shed on the right. The exit from Kidderminster is unremarkable, passing a former sugar beet factory that was the line's last source of freight traffic, but once through a 480-yd (439m) tunnel, the line enters a wholly different landscape. Heathland borders the line until the approach to Bewdley, where you can usually see the animals of West Midlands Safari Park. The home town of the former prime minister Stanley Baldwin is well worth an hour or two's exploration on foot: it has some fine vernacular buildings of medieval and Georgian origin and a remarkably good museum illustrating local crafts such as rope-making and honey farming. The station here was once the junction for lines to Hartlebury and to Tenbury Wells, accounting for its three platforms. Good views of the town and Telford's bridge of 1801 can be had from the eight-arch viaduct to the north of the station.

Colourful sails try to catch the breeze on Trimpley Reservoir, skirted by the railway before it descends through woods to the engineering highlight of the line – the Victoria Bridge. Designed by John Fowler – who later designed the Forth Bridge – and cast by the famous Coalbrookdale Company, the 200-ft (61m) span was the longest cast-iron clear span in the world when it was completed in 1861. It is worth disembarking at the next station, Arley, for a pleasant walk beside the River Severn, which is seldom out of view for the rest of the journey, back to the bridge to admire its construction and its idyllic setting.

The valley of the Severn is remarkably unspoilt as the train presses north through Highley station to Hampton Loade, to which generations of anglers have travelled from Birmingham over the years, and where a river ferry gives access to the opposite bank and its riverside pubs. Beyond the closed halt at Eardington, a bend in the river increases its distance from the line as it traverses a deep cutting and short tunnel. A succession of bridges and viaducts precedes journey's end at Bridgnorth, where the old town can be reached by the footbridge from the station.

LEFT: THE SVR'S KIDDERMINSTER STATION IS A MODERN REPLICA IN TRADITIONAL GWR STYLE.
BELOW: GWR SMALL 4-6-0 NO. 7802 *BRADLEY MANOR* DEPARTS FROM BEWDLEY.

ABOVE LEFT: EMERGING THROUGH CLOUDS OF STEAM FROM ITS CYLINDER DRAIN-COCKS, BR STANDARD 2-6-4T NO. 80079 DEPARTS FROM KIDDERMINSTER.
FAR LEFT: THE VICTORIA BRIDGE AT ARLEY CARRIES TRAINS HIGH ABOVE THE RIVER SEVERN.

Snowdon Mountain Railway
Gwynedd
Llanberis, 6 miles (9.5km) east of Caernarfon

In comparison with the Alps, Britain's peaks are pretty lowly affairs, but the grandeur of Snowdon, the highest mountain in England and Wales, has long attracted the fittest walkers. Until 1896 they were the only people to scale its slopes, but on 6 April 1896 the 2ft 7½ inch (800mm) gauge Snowdon Mountain Railway began operations from Llanberis to the Summit station. It was a sad day for the promoters, for a locomotive derailed and plummeted down the mountainside. Fitting an additional safety device delayed opening for another year, but since then the railway has operated without incident and carried millions of passengers up the mountain.

RIGHT: ASCENDING THE
MOUNTAIN IS ALMOST
LIKE CLIMBING A
STAIRCASE, WITH THE
TWIN RACK RAILS AND
THEIR ASSOCIATED
SAFETY GUIDES

LEFT: THE SNOWDON
MOUNTAIN RAILWAY IS
BRITAIN'S ONLY
EXAMPLE OF A SWISS
RACK-AND-PINION
RAILWAY. THIS WAS THE
ONLY METHOD BY
WHICH TRAINS COULD
ASCEND THE HIGHEST
MOUNTAIN IN WALES.

TRAIN SERVICE

DAILY FROM MID-MARCH TO THE END OF OCTOBER AND ALSO ON SELECTED DATES DURING NOVEMBER AND DECEMBER FOR 'TURKEY AND TINSEL' TRAINS (PRE-BOOKING IS REQUIRED).

TEL: 0870 458 0033

WEBSITE: WWW.SNOWDONRAILWAY.CO.UK

LEFT: LOCOMOTIVE *MOEL SIABOD* TAKES WATER PRIOR TO DESCENDING THE MOUNTAIN.

RIGHT: NEWLY ARRIVED DIESEL POWER GIVES THE RAILWAY MORE OPERATING FLEXIBILITY, BUT LIKE THE STEAM LOCOMOTIVES, IS ALWAYS DEPLOYED AT THE REAR TO PROPEL ITS COACH UP THE MOUNTAIN.

The Snowdon Mountain Railway is Britain's only public rack railway – that is, one equipped with a double-bladed toothed bar between the rails; this is engaged by a cog on the locomotive which claws its way up the mountain. It is worth examining both the pointwork and the mechanism on the steam locomotives to appreciate the skill of the Swiss engineers who built them, based on a system first used in the United States almost 130 years ago and perfected on numerous railways in Switzerland.

The station at Llanberis is close to the ruins of the 13th-century Dolbadarn Castle at the east end of the village. It is advisable to take warm clothing on the 2½-hour round trip, for the weather can change quickly and in severe circumstances the train may not proceed to the summit. But on clear days you can see as far as the Isle of Man and the Wicklow Mountains of Ireland, and the views of the surrounding mountains are breathtaking. For much of the upper section, the railway is built on a ridge, affording a panorama on both sides. All trains now have an in-carriage commentary that plays on the ascent of the mountain. Even before the first public train of the day, a special train with staff and supplies for the summit cafeteria, will have struggled up the mountain. Parts of the line have an average gradient of 1 in 8 and Snowdon Summit, at 3,560ft (1,085m), is the highest point in England and Wales.

Four new acquisitions from Hunslet in Leeds have ended the monopoly of steam on the railway. The diesels enable the railway to provide a more flexible service, responding to a sudden improvement in the weather by laying on more trains. On busy days, it is as well to remember that you are guaranteed a seat only on the train by which you ascended, allowing no more than half an hour on the summit. Ask for details of the 'Early Bird Specials' which offer large discounts on travel for much of the season.

Talyllyn Railway

Gwynedd

Tywyn, 15 miles (24km) west of Machynlleth

TRAIN SERVICE

DAILY FROM LATE MARCH TO OCTOBER, AND SUNDAYS FROM MID-FEBRUARY TO LATE MARCH. SANTA SPECIALS.

TEL: 01654 710472

WEBSITE: WWW.TALYLLYN.CO.UK

It would be hard to overestimate the importance of the Talyllyn Railway in the history of preserved railways throughout the world, for it was the very first such line. The inaugural meeting to save the moribund railway was held in Birmingham in 1950, and a service was run by volunteers from the following year. Its successful formula has been emulated in other countries, from countries as far away as the United States and New Zealand.

But the Talyllyn's distinguished place in the annals of tourist railways might be of little account to today's visitors were it not one of the most characterful of narrow gauge railways. The unusual 2ft 3in (686mm) gauge line threads its way up the south side of the valley of the River Fathew, most of it within the Snowdonia National Park. For much of its length it runs along a shelf in the hillside, affording views across the valley and towards the dominant peak of Cader Idris. But there are also

BELOW: THE ARMORIAL DEVICE OF THE TALYLLYN RAILWAY FEATURES THE PRINCE OF WALES FEATHERS.

wooded sections around Dolgoch (alight for a walk to the falls) and on the final part beyond Abergynolwyn to the terminus at Nant Gwernol.

It was to link the slate quarries at Bryn Eglwys above Nant Gwernol with the main line railway at Tywyn that the railway was originally opened in 1866. At the terminus a new footbridge across the precipitous ravine and woodland trails enables visitors to explore the remains of the quarries and abandoned village.

Besides the charm of its simple stations and the scenery, the Talyllyn Railway is fortunate in having six very different steam locomotives, including the two original to the line, albeit frequently rebuilt. If they seem familiar, it may be because several have been the basis of characters in the Reverend W Awdry's books for children: *Sir Huydn* appears as *Sir Handel*, *Edward Thomas* as *Peter Sam*, *Talyllyn* as *Skarloey* and *Douglas* as *Duncan* in stories about the *Skarloey* (Talyllyn) *Railway*.

It would take an expert to distinguish between the line's original coaches, which are used on Heritage trains during September weekends, and the more recent products of the Talyllyn's carriage works at Pendre. The overall appearance is very similar, but the older vehicles are usually four-wheelers. An exception is the observation car, No 17, which was used on the nearby Corris Railway until 1930, when it was sold for use as a garden shed and greenhouse. Now restored to its original brown livery, it provides the clearest views from the railway during the 55-minute journey.

LEFT: THE 0-4-2T NO 7 *TOM ROLT* COMMEMORATES THE FOUNDING FATHER OF THE PRESERVATION SOCIETY AND IS A CLEVER RECONSTRUCTION OF A 3-FT GAUGE ANDREW BARCLAY 0-4-0WT BUILT FOR THE PEAT BOG RAILWAYS OF IRELAND.

RIGHT: LOCOMOTIVE NO 1 *TALYLLYN* TAKES WATER AT DOLGOCH STATION.

Most passengers join the train at Aberystwyth, where the Vale of Rheidol leaves from a bay platform in the main line station. The days when the Great Western Railway held *thé dansants* on a sprung dance floor at Aberystwyth station are long gone, and it is now the main line that is the poor relation of the preserved railway. Its smartly turned-out trains have at least three times the number of carriages as those bound for Shrewsbury. For much of the 11½-mile (19km) journey the line clings to the hillside on a sinuous ledge with awesome drops below. Views en route are superb with the opening up of viewing breaks in the woodland that flanks the upper part of the line, once spanned by an aerial cableway that brought lead to the station at Rhiwfron. Unless a request stop is made at one of the seven intermediate stations, the four intermediate halts are requested stops only. All uphill trains stop at Nantyronen to take water, and all trains stop at Capel Bangor and Aberffrwd Stations to change tokens. In the high season trains pass at either station.

Time should be allowed to admire the three bridges, one above the other at the summit. They span a whirlpool known as the *Devil's Punchbowl*. The oldest, at the lowest level, was completed by monks in 1087. About 1½ hours should be allowed for a visit to the Mynach waterfalls, which includes steep climbs.

LEFT: NO 9 *PRINCE OF WALES* PAUSES ON THE LOOP AT THE INTERMEDIATE CROSSING STATION OF ABERFFRWD.

Welsh Highland Railway
Caernarfon

The Welsh Highland Railway, as rebuilt, will link two important towns and two coastal regions. In the north, Caernarfon, with its mighty Norman fortress and, in the south, the seaside town and harbour at Porthmadog on Cardigan Bay. In between these two towns lies the Snowdonia National Park.

In the 19th century, Victorian entrepreneurs saw that such a railway link would have great benefits to the area. It wasn't until over a hundred years later that their dream would be realised with the rebuilding of the WHR. Like its sister the Ffestiniog Railway, the WHR is 60cm gauge – much smaller than the standard gauge of most of the world's railways. As you will see on your journey, there are lots of sharp corners on the WHR!

Caernarfon station is near the old slate quays near the castle. The train leaves Caernarfon, climbing a steep gradient, and runs alongside the cycle path, Lon Eifion, with which it shares the old main line trackbed. In the distance, on your right, you can see the three peaks of Yr Eifl on the Llyn Peninsula and, on your left, the mountains of Snowdonia.

Continuing alongside Lon Eifion, the railway climbs past some of the original Nantlle Railway tunnels, under a bridge and into Dinas station. This is the main workshop area of the railway, and many different sorts of wagons can be seen in the sidings. Leaving Dinas you'll see the engine shed. The railway takes a sharp turn to the left and goes under the main road. You are now on the original WHR trackbed for the first time.

The railway passes through attractive fields, some sown with wild flowers by the railway company as part of its commitment to the local ecology. The line snakes around a large farm and under a bridge with the remains of Tryfan Junction station on the right. You can still see the remains of the Bryngwyn branch curving off to the right just after the level crossing – it is hoped that the old branch line will eventually become a footpath. There are views on your left to Caernarfon and Anglesey.

Cefn Du mountain. The train dives under the road bridge and comes into Waunfawr station.

There is a water tank at Waunfawr station and you can often see the locomotive replenishing its water supply. On leaving the station, the train now runs alongside the road to Rhyd Ddu and

The railway now enters the valley of the Afon Gwyrfai and the hills begin to creep in nearer the train. The river is below the railway on the left. Gradually the river becomes visible through the trees as the railway attains the same height above sea level. As the river broadens out and curves off to the left you can see the houses of Waunfawr perched on the hillside of

Beddgelert. The mountain in front, Mynydd Mawr, is known as Elephant Mountain locally as its profile is similar to an elephant!

The train crosses the Afon Gwyrfai on a bridge, passing the remains of the old Betws Garmon station on the right. To your left there is the beautiful church of St. Garmon with a series of adits (mines) like giant steps carved into the hillside.

The train then crosses from the 'right' side of the valley to the 'left' side passing under the road once more next to Castell Cidwm hotel. This is a delightful spot to have a pot of tea by Llyn Cwellyn if you're walking or cycling in the area. There are often small boats on the lake when the weather is fine.

Now the railway starts to climb in earnest as the foothills of Snowdon appear menacingly close on your left. The mountains look enticing on a fine clear day but on a typically damp day with swirling cloud they can be treacherous. It is essential that walkers wear appropriate clothing and carry a map and compass, as the weather can turn very quickly up here.

After passing several farms the railway curves past a barn and arrives at Snowdon Ranger Halt where there is a path to the summit of Snowdon.

Leaving Snowdon Ranger the train gains height above the valley, passing two farms nestling below, before turning sharply to cross the spectacular Glan-yr-afon viaduct. On the left a waterfall is hidden in the trees and to the right the stream cascades down past another farm and into Llyn Cwellyn.

The line now has fine views to your right back down the valley towards Llyn Cwellyn and across to the forestry on the other side at the foot of Mynydd Mawr. Next, the train bends back round in a horseshoe curve and heads directly towards the village of Rhyd Ddu. At the last minute the train turns sharply to the left, over the Snowdon Summit footpath, and into our station. Here there is a car park and a toilet building provided by the National Park. From here you can look up to, and if you're feeling energetic, walk up to, the summit of Snowdon or towards Beddgelert and the imposing bulk of Moel Hebog.

The railway has exciting plans for the future as it has permission under the Transport & Works Act to rebuild the railway all the way through to the headquarters at Harbour Station, Porthmadog.

TRAIN SERVICE

SERVICE: THROUGH MOST OF THE YEAR.

TEL: 01766 516000

WEBSITE: WWW.FESTRAIL.CO.UK

FAR LEFT: SNOWDONIA NATIONAL PARK.

LEFT: CONTRACTORS AND VOLUNTEERS HAVE WORKED SIDE-BY-SIDE TO RECONSTRUCT THE LONG-DEAD RAILWAY.

Welshpool & Llanfair Railway
Powys
Welshpool, 16 miles (25km) west of Shrewsbury

The Welshpool & Llanfair Railway is a survivor of an oddity in Britain – the general purpose narrow gauge railway. The few lines that were built to narrow gauge, mostly in Wales, had a specific traffic to justify their construction, but from its opening in 1903 until closure in 1956, this 2ft-6in (762mm) gauge line carried general merchandise and the district's products, such as livestock, timber and flour. It even carried passengers until bus competition brought that service to an end in 1931.

Unfortunately the section through the large market town of Welshpool, linking with the main line station on the Shrewsbury–Aberystwyth line, ran between the houses and was not available. So the terminus of the 8-mile (13km) line at Llanfair Caereinion became the headquarters.

The locomotives maintained there are an intriguing mix. Besides the two tank engines built for the line, *The Earl* and *The Countess*, there are locomotives rescued from railways in Austria, Finland, West Africa and Antigua as well as other British lines. With some of them came coaches, and a highlight of a 45-minute journey is to stand on the balcony of one of the Austrian coaches as the locomotive tackles the fierce 1 in 29 gradient out of Welshpool.

During recent years the railway has received a Heritage Lottery Grant enabling it to restore both original locomotives to operating condition, restore heritage wagons in order to put on demonstration freight trains at special events and improve passenger facilities at Llanfair Caerenion including a tearoom. A replica of one of the original

RIGHT: *THE COUNTESS* TAKES WATER FROM THE NEWLY INSTALLED PARACHUTE TANK AT WELSHPOOL.

carriages completed during 2004 will enable authentic 1930s mixed passenger and freight trains to be operated.

The scenery is a joy, for the sparsely inhabited pastoral landscape has lost none of its charm under the onslaught of modern agriculture. Woods still cover much of the broad, shallow valley, including the peripheral woodland of the Powis Castle estate, and towards Llanfair you can see the mills that once ground flour beside the River Banwy. The bridge carrying the line over the river nearly spelt disaster to the fledgling preservationists. The winter after the reopening of the line in 1963, storms seriously damaged the bridge, but thanks to help from army engineers and the public response to an appeal fund, the bridge was rebuilt the following summer.

At Llanfair visitors have the opportunity to look at the Welshpool & Llanfair's locomotives and rolling stock, and wonder at the extraordinary contrast between the massive 2-6-2T from the Jokioisten Railway in Finland and the diminutive No 8 *Dougal* which worked at a gasworks in Glasgow. It is hard to believe they run on the same gauge.

LEFT: BOTH ORIGINAL LOCOMOTIVES CROSS THE REBUILT BRIDGE OVER THE RIVER BANWY.

BELOW: THE TINIEST LOCOMOTIVE IS THE FORMER GASWORKS SHUNTER *DOUGAL*.

TRAIN SERVICE

SELECTED DAYS FROM MID-APRIL TO OCTOBER; DAILY FOR SEVEN WEEKS FROM MID-JULY. SANTA SPECIALS.

TEL: 01938 810441

WEBSITE: WWW.WLLR.ORG.UK

TRAIN SERVICE

WEEKENDS AND BANK HOLIDAYS; ALSO WEDNESDAY, THURSDAY, FRIDAY FROM MAY TO SEPTEMBER. SANTA SPECIALS.

TEL: 0161 764 7790

WEBSITE: WWW.EAST-LANCS-RLY.CO.UK

East Lancashire Railway

Greater Manchester/Lancashire

Bury, 6 miles (9.5km) west of Rochdale

This 12-mile (19km) line is an eye-opener to anyone who thinks of the industrial part of Lancashire as being irredeemably spoiled by the past. Following the course of the River Irwell for its whole length, the line passes through the attractive Rossendale Valley with well-wooded hills and a network of footpaths for those who wish to explore the valley. Yet there is hardly a mile of the East Lancashire Railway where sidings did not feed into the line from adjacent mills or quarries. Today, though, you will need someone who knows the area's history, or a good guide book and a sharp eye, to identify their remains, which diminish with each summer's growth. Some cotton mills still stand, but few serve their original purpose and most are converted to flats or are used by small businesses. The days

when the railway tapped these countless sources of traffic and took their products for export all over the world seem almost as remote as the packhorse trains and canal barges that preceded them.

The most interesting and relaxing way to reach the southern terminus of the line at Bury, Bolton Street station is by Metrolink, the light rail network that runs from Altrincham through the centre of Manchester to Bury. The short walk between the two stations can pass the Art Gallery & Museum, which has a remarkable collection of Victorian paintings, including work by Turner. The station at Bolton Street is typical of the secondary town station, with two platforms and loops for through trains. East Lancashire trains may well be hauled by visiting locomotives – as a comparatively recent addition to the ranks of tourist railways, most of its own locomotives from Barry are still under restoration. Departing trains almost immediately enter a short tunnel, its northern portal crenellated to commemorate the medieval castle that was excavated when the tunnel was built.

The railway passes close to Peel Mill, once owned by the Peel family whose best-known member, Robert, became prime minister and founder of the police force – hence 'peelers'. The first station is at Summerseat, an industrial

LEFT: A LIGHTWEIGHT TRAIN HAULED BY AN LMS CLASS 2MT 2-6-0.

RIGHT: A BRITISH RAILWAY STANDARD CLASS 4MT 4-6-0.

village dominated by the East Lancashire Railway's 13-span, 200-yard (183m) Brooksbottom Viaduct. The listed Hoyle Mill is now converted into luxury flats, and the adjacent mill offices and pump room are now a pub and restaurant.

The second tunnel after Summerseat has an unusual north portal: Nuttall Tunnel was built at the insistence of the owner of Nuttall Hall so that the railway would not impede his view of the river. The East Lancashire's directors decided to make a virtue out of necessity and created an elaborate turretted and crenellated face to the tunnel, into which were set what are thought to be carved faces of the directors. The expanse of Nuttall Park can be seen to the east as you cross a 275-yard (251m) girder viaduct. The Grant family that lived at Nuttall Hall was immortalised by Charles Dickens as the Cheeryble Brothers in *Nicholas Nickleby*. The park, now publicly owned, can be easily visited on foot from the next station at Ramsbottom. The town is worth exploring with the help of a leaflet for a walk that takes in the Ramsbottom Heritage Centre and other sites of interest. There are also walks up Holcombe Hill to the commemorative Peel Tower, with various pubs en route.

Leaving Ramsbottom the train passes the site of extensive sidings and runs along an embankment with the river on the right. The valley narrows before the former junction at Stubbins where the main line to Accrington continued straight ahead, while the East Lancashire swings to the right. It appears that the line is dropping down, but this illusion is caused simply by the steeper gradient of the Accrington line to the west – in fact the East Lancashire line climbs steadily all the way from Bury to journey's end at Rawtenstall. Look out for the imposing Alberbottom Viaduct on the Accrington line: its poor structural condition ended proposals to reopen this route.

Isle of Man Steam Railway
Douglas
Isle of Man

LEFT: BEYER PEACOCK 2-4-0T NO.4 *LOCH* ON THE STEEP CLIMB OUT OF DOUGLAS. RIGHT: TRADITIONAL IMR LIVERIES HAVE BECOME POPULAR AGAIN.

For a small island of 220 square miles (570 sq km), the Isle of Man is well blessed with railways. The Manx Electric Railway continues in its second century of operation to perform an important function, linking Douglas with Ramsey. The Snaefell Mountain Railway takes visitors to the 2,036-foot (621m) summit; and the island's newest railway, the Groudle Glen, is a reconstruction of the Victorian railway that took visitors to a sea lion pool and bear pit, using one of the original locomotives. But those in search of steam head for the 3-foot (900mm) gauge Isle of Man Steam Railway, running from Douglas to Port Erin.

The 15-mile (24km) line is the last route of the Isle of Man Railway that once also served Peel, Foxdale and Ramsey. Even this remnant nearly closed, but the more farsighted members of Tynwald, the island's parliament, urged its retention and in 1976 the government agreed to buy it.

The railway is now an intrinsic part of the island's tourist industry, and the Year of the Railway celebrations in 1993 brought tens of thousands to the island to ride on the various lines and trains. The reason for that enthusiasm is easy to understand as you will be hauled by one of the original little tank engines. The carriages are also original Isle of Man stock, though many have been rebuilt or reupholstered.

The station is still imposing, built like others on the Port Erin line in the distinctive Ruabon brick, but it is no longer easy to see how the station once handled 100 trains a day, since the platforms have been reduced in number. The 65-minute journey is as delightful as ever, the steep gradients of the line reflecting the rolling hills and eliciting a vigorous exhaust beat from the locomotive. Before Port Soderick, passengers enjoy views over the coast and can disembark to visit the beach and cove. Passing through woods you reach Castletown with its medieval fortress of Castle Rushen, before the unspoiled town of Port Erin. The station here offers a museum about the railway, and good cakes in the station tearoom.

ABOVE: ISLE OF MAN RAILWAY CREST. RIGHT: NIGHT PHOTOGRAPHY IS POPULAR.

TRAIN SERVICE

DAILY FROM APRIL TO OCTOBER. SANTA SPECIALS.

TEL: 01624 662525/663366

WEBSITE: WWW.GOV.IM/TOURISM

The National Railway Museum, York

Preserved railways are wonderful at re-creating the atmosphere of the steam railway and at giving those who have never seen a steam engine at work an idea of their appeal. But what they cannot do is to place railways in an economic and social context. For a lively introduction to the way railways have developed from rudimentary beginnings and changed the world, the National Railway Museum cannot be bettered.

Only ten minutes' walk from York station, the museum is now the largest railway museum in the world. It opened in 1975 following the amalgamation of the earlier small museum at York with the large collection from Clapham in London. A major expansion opened in 1992, allowing exhibits to be placed in a more authentic setting in the station hall, once the North Eastern Railway goods shed.

The displays illustrate the way the experience and quality of train travel has evolved by matching locomotives and carriages of the same period and surrounding them with contemporary artefacts. This has allowed the displays in the original Great Hall to concentrate on the technology of railways, presenting items which try to foster an understanding of the various components of the railway.

In 1999, a new £4-million wing, known as The Works was opened; it has many interactive displays and sections on track and signalling show how the quest for safety has driven innovation and made railways by far the safest form of land transport.

A reconstruction of Wolverton works manager's office is part of an introduction to the absorbing subject of railway workers, from navvy to general manager.

The impact of railways on the carriage of mail, on royal travelling habits, holidays, civil engineering and steamer services are all presented in imaginative displays that convey their information in a light and interesting way. But the greatest space is devoted to locomotives and rolling stock, of which the museum has an unparalleled collection, ranging from a working replica of *Rocket* to the prototype High Speed Train power car, from the horse-drawn carriage of 1863 that worked at Port Carlisle to the royal saloon built in 1941 for HM Queen Elizabeth, the late Queen Mother. A star attraction is inevitably the world's fastest steam locomotive, *Mallard*, which topped 126mph (201kph), and there is a cutaway locomotive which shows the inner workings of a steam engine.

The museum has a lively programme of events embracing audio-visual and film displays, theatrical enactments, great moments in railway history, photography and painting exhibitions and Days Out With *Thomas* to mention just a few, so regular visitors will always find something new to interest them.

In 2003 the NRM won its second award for excellence. Recent exhibits include a Japanese Shinkansen Bullet Train which arrived in 2001, whilst in the summer of 2004 a Railfest extravaganza was put on to celebrate rail's bicentenary, as the world's first steam locomotive emerged from a Welsh ironworks in 1804.

The range of exhibits and the stories behind them are so diverse and of such historical significance that the museum has an education service with a pre-bookable teaching programme for schools and an interactive learning centre.

NRM is the world's largest railway museum and the exhibits are so vividly displayed that it would be difficult to be disappointed by a visit. There is truly something for every one. Admission is free but there are charges for special events such as 'Thomas' and 'Railfest'. The museum is open daily except 24th to 26th December. Telephone 01904 621261 or visit the website www.nrm.org.uk

ABOVE: THE WORKING REPLICA OF GEORGE STEPHENSON'S *ROCKET* TAKES PRIDE OF PLACE.

ABOVE: *GLADSTONE* IS THE FOCUS OF ATTENTION ON THE TURNTABLE.

RIGHT: EAST AND WEST COAST EXPRESS LOCOMOTIVES STAND SIDE BY SIDE AT YORK. ON THE LEFT THE STREAMLINED LNER A4 CLASS *MALLARD* HOLDS THE WORLD SPEED RECORD FOR STEAM.

Keighley & Worth Valley Railway
West Yorkshire
Keighley, 9 miles (14.5km) west of Bradford

TRAIN SERVICE
DAILY FROM JUNE TO THE END OF AUGUST, AND WEEKENDS THROUGHOUT THE YEAR.
TEL: 01535 647777/645214
WEBSITE: WWW.KWVR.CO.UK

After a journey on the Keighley & Worth Valley Railway, it's hard to believe that the line is only 4 miles (6.5km) long – it feels twice that length. It may be the three-and-a-half intermediate stations or the twisting valley that delude the senses, but the railway offers visitors much more than its length would suggest. This is one of the oldest standard gauge preserved railways, having opened to passengers six weeks before the end of steam on British railways in 1968, and six years after the line was closed down. The society that still runs the railway – one of the most democratic of any preserved railway – came into being when the late Bob Cryer, MP, called a public meeting soon after closure to passengers.

What really put the line on the map was its use for the filming of *The Railway Children* in 1969. Based on the novel by E Nesbit, and starring Jenny Agutter and Bernard Cribbins, the film brought tens of thousands of visitors to the railway. Its unique atmosphere and its wide range of stock has ensured the frequent use of the railway by film and television companies, notably the use of Keighley for the emotional departure scene in *Yanks* with Richard Gere.

One of the advantages of being in the vanguard of railway preservation was that the Keighley & Worth Valley and its supporting societies were able to acquire some choice examples of both locomotives and rolling stock. Amongst them are carriages built as long ago as the 1870s, such as the Lancashire & Yorkshire Railway Directors' Saloon and the beautifully restored Great Central Railway four-wheeled coach in which HRH The Duchess of York has travelled. Such gems are used only on special occasions, but even the most modern carriage on the railway dates from 1961. At Ingrow, the Museum of Rail Travel is the home of the Vintage Carriage Trust and houses perhaps the finest collection of historic coaches in the country. The museum is open every day except Christmas Day and entry is free to all KWVR Day Rover ticket holders. Ingrow, Haworth and Oxenhope stations all have large car parks.

Most journeys begin at Keighley, which can be reached by frequent West Yorkshire Metro trains from Leeds and Bradford. Other than a renewal of signs, little seems to have changed on platform four since the Midland Railway rebuilt the whole of Keighley station in 1883. The period W H Smith outlet shelters under the ornately bracketed canopy that follows the gentle curve of the platform as it points up the valley. This curve, compounded by the 1 in 66 gradient, proved the undoing of the

LEFT: THE PLATFORM AT HAWORTH, THE RAILWAY'S HEADQUARTERS. RIGHT: THE GWR PANNIER TANK NO. 5775 WITH THE LIVERY USED IN THE FILM *THE RAILWAY CHILDREN*.

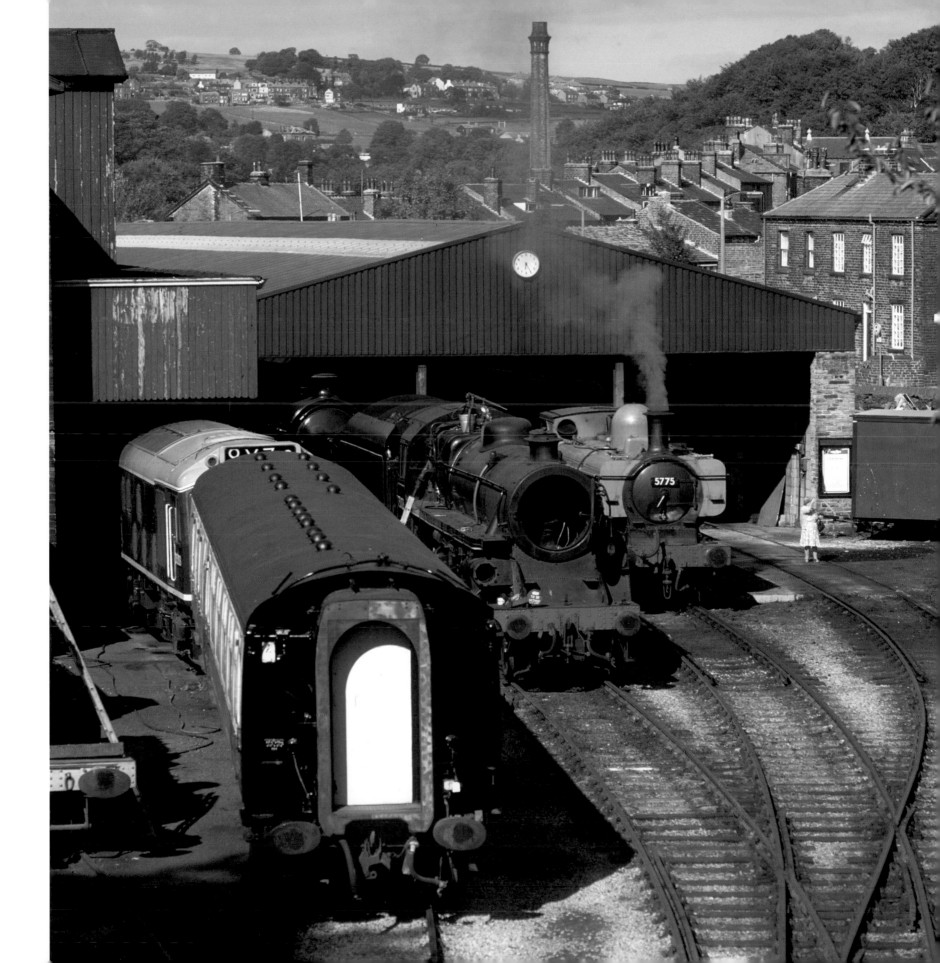

opening train in 1867, which slipped ignominiously to a standstill. The resourceful driver, however, reversed right through the station to take a good run at it and conquered the slope without further embarrassment.

The climb to Ingrow is still a test for engine crews, and the line continues to climb all the way to Oxenhope. Some of the mills that provided much of the line's goods traffic can still be seen here and there up the valley, but many have gone.

Ingrow station has been transformed since the early 1980s when it had a derelict air, the original vandalised station having been demolished. Thanks principally to the generosity of a

ABOVE: THE RISING GRADIENT FROM KEIGHLEY TO OXENHOPE MEANS THE SMALLER LOCOMOTIVES, SUCH AS LMS *JINTY* 0-6-0T NO 47279 HAVE TO WORK HARD. LEFT: THE FIREMAN ALSO WORKS HARD UP THE WORTH VALLEY.

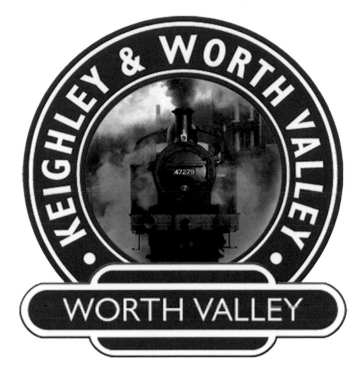

Oxenhope that follows the railway, crossing a 17th-century packhorse bridge and affording sight of Three Chimneys, used as the home of *The Railway Children*. Walkers can enjoy refreshments at Oxenhope and look round the museum, where some of the line's most historic vehicles and locomotives are kept, before taking the train home from the delightful station.

LEFT: THE WORTH VALLEY LOGO EMBODIES THE GRAPHIC STYLES OF THE 1950S.

BELOW: BR STANDARD CLASS 4MT NO 75070 WAS RESCUED IN SCRAP CONDITION BUT IS NOW A STAR PERFORMER ON THE WORTH VALLEY RAILWAY.

society member, a Midland Railway stone station building in Lancashire was dismantled and re-erected here, oil lamps were installed and the stout entrance gates were recovered from a Keighley goods yard when it was replaced by a supermarket.

Pausing briefly at the request stop of Damems, reputedly the smallest railway station in Britain, the train soon enters Damems passing loop, specially put in by the Keighley & Worth Valley Railway to increase the number of trains that can be operated. Pasture edged with stone walls and well dotted with trees, the railway climbs to Oakworth station, where Mr Perks held court in *The Railway Children*. The gas lamps, enamelled advertising signs, milk churns and the superbly restored interior make the station a period delight. The train soon reaches one of the favourite places for photographers, the three-arch Mytholmes Viaduct seen from the top of the tunnel of the same name and the scene of several sequences in that memorable film.

After passing the huge mass of Ebor Mill, you reach Haworth, where many leave the train either to visit the locomotive shed and workshops or to explore the home town of the Brontë sisters. The enduring fascination of the literary family has made the mill town a major tourist attraction.

There is a lovely walk between Haworth and the terminus at

Lakeside & Haverthwaite Railway

Cumbria

Staveley, 9 miles (14.5km) south of Windermere

LEFT: EVERY DEPARTURE FROM HAVERTHWAITE IS A BOAT TRAIN, CONNECTING WITH THE LAKE STEAMERS AT LAKESIDE. THIS IS ONE OF THE LMS FAIRBURN TANKS HURRYING THROUGH THE LAKELAND LANDSCAPE.

It is a cruel irony that the Lake Poets, and in particular Wordsworth, created a fascination for the romantic beauty of the district and then felt compelled to turn their pens to resisting the means whereby large numbers could enjoy it. However, it was the other railway to reach the shore of Windermere, the still open Kendal & Windermere, that was the subject of a vitriolic poem by Wordsworth. By the time the Furness Railway reached Lakeside in 1869, Wordsworth had been dead for 19 years.

The headquarters of the 3-mile (5km) Lakeside & Haverthwaite Railway is at the latter station, curiously positioned between two unlined tunnels, like the bizarrely sited stations beside the Ligurian Sea between Genoa and La Spezia. The original idea was to connect with the main railway line farther south at Plympton, but a road-widening scheme put paid to it. The tank locomotives that operate the line have a stiff climb out of Haverthwaite, running

parallel with a line that served Backbarrow Ironworks until it closed in 1967. The finest views are over the Leven Valley to the east of the line, with the river frequently in sight. A large factory producing ultramarine (Reckitt's Blue) is passed on the right, and – more picturesquely – a waterfall and adjacent mill can be seen before the small halt at Newby Bridge is reached. It was while staying at the Newby Bridge Hotel in 1931 that Arthur Ransome wrote *Swallows and Amazons*. The halt, used during World War II to bring prisoners to the Grizedale Hall prisoner-of-war camp, is the start of a number of fine walks. But visitors should not miss the section of the line from here to Lakeside for it is the most scenic part, passing through oakwoods and skirting the southern end of Lake Windermere.

The station buildings provided by the Furness Railway for its train and steamer services at Lakeside were so splendid that some shareholders complained of extravagance. Sadly

they were almost entirely demolished before the Lakeside & Haverthwaite took over. However, steamers still connect with trains for a 3-hour cruise of the lake, which can be prolonged by visiting the Windermere Steam Boat Museum. Amongst the elegant vessels in its collection is the steam yacht *Esperance*, which Arthur Ransome immortalised as the houseboat in *Swallows and Amazons*.

ABOVE: THE FAIRBURN 2-6-4 TANKS HAVE HAD DIFFERENT LIVERIES SINCE 1973, BUT NOW HAVE THEIR 1950s BRITISH RAILWAYS APPEARANCE.

TRAIN SERVICE

EASTER WEEK AND APRIL WEEKENDS, THEN DAILY FROM LATE APRIL TO OCTOBER.

TEL: 015395 31594

WEBSITE: WWW.LAKESIDERAILWAY.CO.UK

North Yorkshire Moors Railway

North Yorkshire

Pickering, 16 miles (25km) west of Scarborough

The appreciation of landscapes may be subjective, but few would argue with the claim that the scenery enjoyed by visitors to the North Yorkshire Moors Railway is some of the finest on any preserved railway. Moreover, the 18-mile (29km) railway can be reached by the charming Network Rail branch line that runs from the shadows of the transporter bridge at Middlesbrough through Eskdale to Whitby. The interchange at Grosmont is almost across the platform.

If you are not arriving by rail, there is more parking space available at Pickering, and the nearby Beck Isle Museum provides an introduction to life on the North York Moors. The attractive stone station building is the first of many fine period structures on the line, including goods sheds and signal boxes. The only note of incongruity is the bizarre use of colour light signals at Pickering.

For the first two-thirds of the hour-long journey, the railway closely follows the course of Pickering Beck through roadless Newton Dale. This unspoiled valley was scoured out by glacial action and offers walkers many opportunities, which are indicated on information boards at Levisham and Newtondale stations. Soon after the train leaves the passing loop at Levisham, to the right you will see the architectural folly of Skelton Tower, erected by an eccentric Victorian vicar of the same name. The steep climb up the valley continues to an isolated farmhouse shortly before Newtondale Halt, where passengers need to request the train to stop. A waymarked path leads through the woods to the west of the line back to Levisham station. Beyond the Halt the gradient eases briefly as the train leaves the forest behind and enters a section of dramatic open moorland. After the Summit, at Fen Bog, there are brief views of the early

LEFT: AGAINST THE SETTING OF THOMAS PROSSER'S STONE-BUILT STATION AT GOATHLAND, FORMER LAMBTON RAILWAY 0-6-2T NO 29 PREPARES TO TAKE ITS TRAIN ON TO GROSMONT. RIGHT: THE NORTH EASTERN RAILWAY 0-8-0 HEAVY FREIGHT ENGINE NO 2238 SETTING OFF FROM LEVISHAM.

TRAIN SERVICE

USUALLY FOR A WEEK AT FEBRUARY HALF-TERM, THEN DAILY FROM LATE MARCH TO LATE OCTOBER. SANTA SPECIALS ON WEEKENDS BEFORE CHRISTMAS, WITH A FINAL FEW DAYS OVER THE NEW YEAR.

TEL: 01751 472508/473535

WEBSITE: WWW.NORTHYORKSHIREMOORSRAILWAY.COM

LEFT: NER 0-6-0 NO. 65894 AND LAMBTON TANK NO. 29 DRAW THEIR TRAIN INTO GOATHLAND STATION.

RIGHT: A SOUTHERN REBUILT BULLEID LIGHT PACIFIC ATTACKS THE GRADIENT ABOVE BECK HOLE.

warning station at Fylingdales, where a pyramid structure replaced the earlier 'golf balls'.

At Eller Beck the line is crossed by the Lyke Wake Walk, which links the coast at Ravenscar with Osmotherley. The observant eye will detect traces of an abandoned railway formation on the west side of the line, which was the course of the railway until 1865 when the present line was built to eliminate a major hindrance to the railway – the inclined plane from Goathland down to Beck Hole near Grosmont. Horses and then locomotives had to haul carriages and wagons to the foot and summit of this incline, which was operated at first by a water balanced arrangement and later powered by a stationary steam engine. It is well worth breaking your journey at Goathland – the station is the most attractive on the line, with some fine North Eastern Railway signals and an award-winning conversion of the former goods shed to a tearoom with seating in restored wagons. A booklet describing the 3-mile (5km) Rail Trail to Grosmont is available from the station

shop. There are many other attractive walks around this moorland village: one of the longer routes, for which boots are desirable, takes you past the celebrated Mallyan Spout waterfall and one of the best-preserved stretches of Roman road, on Wheeldale Moor. The descent of the line to Grosmont is one of the loveliest sections, dropping down through the woods and criss-crossing Eller Beck before it joins the Murk Esk at Beck Hole. The noise and smoke of ascending trains as they struggle up the fearsome 1 in 49 gradient is one of the most stirring sounds and sights to be enjoyed on a preserved railway. A little exploration, aided by a suitable map, will reveal some excellent photographic viewpoints – without any need to trespass on the line!

As you near Grosmont, the long line of the Esk Valley cottages – built for iron-stone miners in the late 19th century – and the trackbed of the old line (now part of the Rail Trail) can be seen to the left. Soon after, the railway's locomotive workshops and depot can be seen on the right, with a rare example of a mechanical coaling plant built since the end of steam on British railways. A whistle from the locomotive and you plunge into the double track tunnel that brings the train to a second bridge over the Murk Esk and journey's end – unless you are changing to a train bound for Whitby. But if you have time, take a walk through George Stephenson's original 1836 tunnel to see at close quarters the locomotives in or around the sheds.

The history of this railway is particularly interesting. The Whitby & Pickering was an early line, built by the 'father of British railways', George Stephenson, and opened with the noisy celebration of five bands and 7,000 people in 1836. A book in tribute to the railway was even published in the same year – *The Scenery of the Whitby & Pickering Railway* – illustrated by G. H. Dodgson who was apprenticed to Stephenson. Charles Dickens was amongst the early travellers on the 'quaint old railway', commenting on the use of horses for part of the way.

About twenty steam locomotives and over a dozen diesels are based on the railway but it is very unlikely that all will be present together at the same time. Working locomotives visit other railways and centres from time to time while some may be elsewhere for overhaul. One NYMR-based engine is often taken to Fort William in the west of Scotland in the summer, so it can operate the 'Jacobite' steam trains to Mallaig. The railway does, however, operate most of its working steam locomotives at gala weekends.

Likewise, other locomotives visit the railway. *Sir Nigel Gresley*, the famous streamlined LNER 'A4' has had a major overhaul at Grosmont after frequent use during recent summer seasons.

The railway publishes a comprehensive Stock Book and periodic amendment sheets recording important changes and details of visiting motive power.

Ravenglass & Eskdale Railway

Cumbria

Ravenglass, 16 miles (25km) south of Whitehaven

It would be hard to quibble with the claim of the Ravenglass & Eskdale Railway that no other miniature railway in Britain passes through such magnificent scenery.

Its origins go back to 1875 when a line was opened from the old Roman port of Ravenglass to haematite mines in Eskdale. Both mines and railway were soon in financial difficulties, but the latter soldiered on, carrying both freight and passengers until 1913.

That would have been the end of the 'Ratty', as it has long been known locally, had it not been for the Northampton

RIGHT: THE 2-6-2 LOCOMOTIVE *NORTHERN ROCK*, BUILT IN THE R&ER'S OWN WORKSHOPS IN 1976, APPROACHES IRTON ROAD.

LEFT: ANOTHER OF HENRY GREENLY'S OUTSTANDING MINIATURE LOCOMOTIVES, *RIVER ESK*.

model engineer and architect W. J. Bassett-Lowke. He leased the line, reduced the gauge from 3ft (900mm) to 15in (375mm) and reopened it to tourists and later to stone traffic. Despite some serious ups and downs since then, its future has been secured because enough people delight in its character, which in large measure stems from the beauty of Eskdale.

Most people begin their journey at the Ravenglass end, which can be reached by train from either Carlisle or from Carnforth and Barrow-in-Furness; both lines hug the coast and are highly recommended. The Ravenglass & Eskdale has almost taken over the main line station at Ravenglass – the main building is a pub, the Ratty Arms, the waiting room on the opposite platform is a museum about the railway's history, and the goods shed has been converted into workshops.

ABOVE: A TRACKSIDE GRADIENT POST.

Trains for the 40-minute journey to Dalegarth/Eskdale leave from the adjacent three-platform station. You pass the signal box – which pioneered radio signalling in Britain – more workshops, the engine shed and the new carriage shed as the train leaves Ravenglass and heads for the first halt at Muncaster Mill. In the distance can be seen another first – the world's first atomic power station at Calder Hall, now Sellafield. The River Mite accompanies the train on its approach to Muncaster Mill and farm. Flour has been ground on this site since at least 1455, though today's renovated structure dates from about 1700.

The railway's six steam locomotives date from 1900 to 1976 and have to be capable of hauling up to 25-ton trains on the steep gradients, some as severe as 1 in 42. The oldest, *Bonnie Dundee*, was built for Dundee's gasworks and has had to be regauged, but the veteran is *Synolda*. This octogenarian from Bassett-Lowke's works dates from 1912 and was the first 15in (380mm) gauge Ravenglass & Eskdale locomotive. It is used only on special occasions, lacking the power and relative youth of the other original engines.

During winter weekdays the railway journey starts from Eskdale, reflecting the importance of any public transport to the remote valley community.

TRAIN SERVICE

DAILY FROM EASTER TO OCTOBER; WEEKENDS IN NOVEMBER AND FEBRUARY; NO SERVICE IN JANUARY. SANTA SPECIALS IN DECEMBER.

TEL: 01229 717171

WEBSITE: WWW.RAVENGLASS-RAILWAY.CO.UK

ABOVE: *NORTHERN ROCK* AND *RIVER IRT* TOGETHER ON THE LOOP AT IRTON ROAD.

LEFT: BAGNALL 0-4-0ST *PETER* ON THE 2FT-GAUGE LINE AT THE AMBERLEY WORKING MUSEUM.

Narrow Gauge Railways

BELOW: THE SOUTH TYNEDALE RAILWAY.

Britain had fewer public narrow gauge railways than any other country in Europe, so many of those that are open to tourists today carried no other passengers than the workmen connected with the industry for which the railway had been built.

Almost every kind of mineral traffic spawned narrow gauge lines, and such railways were even built for sugar beet and potatoes. The 2ft 6in (762mm) gauge Sittingbourne & Kemsley Light Railway was built in 1906 to carry pulp and finished products between a dock on the River Swale and the huge paper mill at Sittingbourne in Kent. Today some of the line's original locomotives haul passengers along the route. In other cases, a railway has been laid in an appropriate setting to illustrate past practice. At The Amberley Working Museum near Arundel, a 2ft (600mm) gauge line has been laid on the 36-acre (14.5ha) site to carry visitors in authentic workmen's vehicles by a variety of steam and diesel locomotives.

Another line that never carried passengers was the Leighton Buzzard Railway in Bedfordshire, which connected sand quarries with the nearest standard gauge branch line. Its collection of locomotives includes a vertical-boilered de Winton, looking rather like an oversized tea urn on wheels, and an engine that spent its life at a pumping station in Calcutta. The firm ride of the home-built carriages is part of the experience.

Some narrow gauge lines have been built on the trackbed of a former standard gauge railway. The Teifi Valley Railway at Llandysul is a 2ft (600mm) gauge line that is built on the bed of the branch to Newcastle Emlyn at Henllan station. Several tank engines operate the line the oldest having been built in 1894. The picturesque standard gauge branch line that ran from England's highest market town of Alston to a junction on the Newcastle–Carlisle line provides the basis of the South Tynedale Railway. Also of 2ft (600mm) gauge, it runs for 2 miles (3km). The railway has locomotives from Natal, Poland, Spain and Germany.

The Groudle Glen Railway on the Isle of Man is a reconstruction of the 2ft (610mm) line that ran in a spectacular cliff-top location to a menagerie. It even has one of the original locomotives – a Bagnall tank engine of 1896.

RIGHT: BLACKSMITHS ARE NEEDED TO MAKE NEW PARTS TO KEEP ENGINES STEAMING.

ABOVE: HQ OF THE SITTINGBOURNE & KEMSLEY LIGHT RAILWAY.

LEFT: THE WHIPSNADE RAILWAY COMBINES THE ATTRACTIONS OF STEAM TRAVEL WITH CLOSE PROXIMITY TO EXOTIC WILDLIFE.

Tanfield Railway

County Durham

Tanfield, 6 miles (9.5km) southwest of
Newcastle-upon-Tyne

Few preserved railways can rival the Tanfield Railway for claims to historical fame – it is the world's oldest working railway and offers passengers sight of the world's oldest surviving railway bridge. These attributes are a clue to the railway's past, for the earliest railways, usually horse-drawn wagonways, were nearly all built to carry coal, in this case from the pits of County Durham to waiting colliers on the River Tyne.

Thought to have been opened in stages between 1712 and 1725, the railway later became a steam-worked branch of the North Eastern Railway. Its industrial ancestry is perfectly reflected in the large number of industrial tank engines based at Marley Hill shed, close to the main station at Andrews House. Many operated on the dense network of colliery lines that bisected the northeast. The oldest, and a regular performer on the Tanfield Railway, was built in nearby Gateshead as long ago as 1873 – few preserved railways can field such a veteran, and no other railway can match the antiquity of the Tanfield's carriages, all of which date from the 19th century.

A ride on the Tanfield Railway is a corrective to those who think of industrial landscapes as being irredeemably ugly – the section between the stone platforms and station building at Andrews House and the southern terminus at East Tanfield is through a deepening gorge lined with oak trees and a smattering of beech, ash and silver birch. It is worth getting off the train at Causey, or returning by the

RIGHT: FORMER
NATIONAL COAL
BOARD AUSTERITY
SADDLETANK NO 49.

network of paths through the woods, to admire both the massive embankment leading to the Causey Arch and the bridge itself. When the latter was built between 1725 and 1727, it was compared with the Via Appia, the greatest Roman road in Italy, and celebrated in prints. It is not hard to understand why people came from all over the country to see the bridge; its single 150ft (46m) arch soars 80ft (24m) above the Causey Burn in a setting worthy of a

landscape painting, and it remained the largest single-span bridge in Britain for 30 years.

The reason for the railway's preservation lies in the survival of the engine shed at Marley Hill, which until 1970 maintained locomotives from the area's colliery railways, despite the closure of the rest of the Tanfield Railway in 1962. The stone building was put up in 1855 and is thought to be the oldest engine shed in the world still fulfilling its original function. So authentic is the atmosphere in its machine shop that it has been used as a setting in the filming of a Catherine Cookson novel. Despite the complete disappearance of the surrounding coke works, colliery and rows of miners' houses at Marley Hill, the Tanfield Railway continues to evoke the true character of the industrial railway in a way that few other preserved railways can.

TRAIN SERVICE

SUNDAYS AND BANK HOLIDAY MONDAYS FROM JANUARY TO NOVEMBER; ALSO WEDNESDAYS AND THURSDAYS FROM MID-JULY TO EARLY SEPTEMBER. SANTA TRAINS OPERATE THROUGHOUT DECEMBER.

TEL: 0191 3887545

WEBSITE: WWW.TANFIELD-RAILWAY.CO.UK

ABOVE: THE TRADITIONAL WORKSHOPS AT MARLEY HILL ARE CAPABLE OF COMPLETE LOCOMOTIVE OVERHAULS. HERE, A PAIR OF DRIVING WHEELS ARE TURNED ON THE WHEEL LATHE.

LEFT: INTERSPERSED BETWEEN THE PASSENGER TRAINS ARE DEMONSTRATION RUNS WITH FREIGHT ROLLING STOCK, WHICH EMPHASISE THE TANFIELD RAILWAY'S INDUSTRIAL ROOTS.

FAR LEFT: TRAINS PASS AT ANDREWS HOUSE STATION.

Bo'ness & Kinneil Railway
Falkirk
Bo'ness, 15 miles (24km) west of Edinburgh

TRAIN SERVICE

EVERY SATURDAY AND SUNDAY FROM EARLY APRIL TO END OF OCTOBER; AND DAILY FROM START OF JULY TO END OF AUGUST. SANTA SPECIALS.

TEL: 01506 825855
TALKING TIMETABLE: 01506 822298

WEBSITE: WWW.SRPS.ORG.UK

The closure of railways in Britain has seldom been accompanied by sensible provisions to safeguard the integrity of the trackbed and structures in case they were needed again. Nonetheless, most railway preservation schemes were on the scene quickly enough to prevent the principal buildings being demolished or sold off. A notable exception was the Bo'ness & Kinneil Railway on the southern shore of the Firth of Forth – when the preservationists began work, they lacked even the remains of the trackbed or any foundations on which to rebuild a working railway.

It is a measure of their achievement that Bo'ness station deceives most visitors into thinking that it is the original. The setting is striking: inland the town of stone buildings rises up the hillside, crowned by the villas of the more well-to-do; seaward

BELOW LEFT: THE B&KR HAS THE FINEST COLLECTION OF SCOTTISH RAILWAY LOCOMOTIVES. BELOW: FORMER NORTH BRITISH RAILWAY 0-6-0 NO. 673 *MAUDE* SHUNTS ROLLING STOCK PAST BO'NESS SIGNAL BOX.

RIGHT: A CALEDONIAN RAILWAY ENSEMBLE: 0-4-4T NO. 419 BUILT IN 1907 AND 1921 BOGIE COACHES.

are the remains of the harbour on which the town's wealth was largely based. At one time 11 miles (18km) of sidings covered the waterfront, the wagons filled with coal for export or with imported iron ore and timber. Today the site is home to the largest collection of historic locomotives, carriages and wagons in Scotland, where most of them were built or worked.

The largest building is the cast- and wrought-iron train shed, built in 1842 for Haymarket station in Edinburgh. The rescue of what is one of the finest buildings on any preserved railway was part of the intention to re-create an authentic North British Railway station – that pre-grouping company owned the line that linked Bo'ness with the Edinburgh–Glasgow main line at Manuel. Other buildings are the station offices from Wormit, at the end of the Tay Bridge, and the signalbox from Garnqueen South Junction, the point near Coatbridge where the Caledonian company's main line to the north diverged from the alignment of the pioneering Monkland & Kirkintilloch Railway.

Before boarding the train or after you have returned, the Scottish Railway Exhibition demands your attention. The exhibition's vast sheds showcase the largest display of railway equipment outside the national museums, together with a well-illustrated display on the history and unique characteristics of railways in Scotland.

Pride of place amongst the carriages must go to the Great North of Scotland Railway saloon which was once part of Edward VII's royal train. However, most of the carriages illustrate just how spartan travelling conditions were for third-class passengers until the early years of this century. Locomotives range from main line passenger engines to humble industrial tank engines from the days when large factories and works would be rail connected and have a 'pug', as they were called in Scotland, fussing round the yard. The glory of the display is in fact the humble wagon, in huge quantity and variety, illustrating how diverse is the railway's service to industry. There is a working colour light signalling display, and a demonstration workshop where current conservation work-in-progress is on view.

The start of the 3½-mile (5.6km) journey to Birkhill, the present terminus of the line, passes the dock on the right before the train meanders through a plantation of saplings that now covers the foreshore. Kinneil Halt is used by birdwatchers

FAR LEFT: *MAUDE*
ACCELERATES ITS TRAIN
ALONG THE
FORESHORE AT BO'NESS
AT THE START OF ITS
JOURNEY TO BIRKHILL.

LEFT: CALEDONIAN
TANK NO. 419 BRINGS
ITS TRAIN INTO
BIRKHILL STATION.

visiting the adjacent bird sanctuary on the headland. The line forges inland, the deepening bark from the locomotive's exhaust indicating the rising gradient.

As the line enters a woodland of ivy-clad trees, it passes close to Kinneil House where an outbuilding was the scene of James Watt's early experiments to produce more efficient steam engines. The sight of Grangemouth oil refinery on the flood plane of the Forth soon disappears from view as the line swings inland and crosses the site of the Antonine Wall, built by the Romans as a bulwark against invasion by the Caledonians. A mile of pastoral landscape precedes arrival at Birkhill, a remote station seemingly offering visitors nothing more than the pretty

station building with its oversized cast iron brackets supporting the canopy. However, simply to return by the next train would be to miss one of the most interesting experiences to be had from a journey on a preserved railway. Behind the station, hidden by trees, are the remains of the surface buildings of Birkhill Fireclay Mine — unremarkable to all except industrial archaeologists, but beyond is an extraordinary sight. The ground drops away to reveal a precipitous gorge through which the River Avon flows. Retired miners now take parties through some of the workings.

Back at Bo'ness, there is a modest shop, and a buffet where you may rest awhile.

Mull & West Highland Narrow Gauge Railway

Argyll & Bute

Craignure, Isle of Mull, near ferry landing from Oban

TRAIN SERVICE

DURING THE EASTER HOLIDAY, THEN DAILY FROM LATE APRIL TO MID-OCTOBER.

TEL: 01680 812494

WEBSITE: WWW.MULLRAIL.CO.UK

Most miniature gauge railways are purely for fun, and often run in circuits. The man credited with their invention, Sir Arthur Heywood, envisaged them being useful for estate or military purposes, but he would have approved of the 10¼-in (260mm) gauge Mull & West Highland Railway – Scotland's only island railway connects with the ferry from Oban to take passengers to one of the island's principal tourist attractions, the mid-19th century Torosay Castle. The connections are generous, allowing passengers half an hour to find their land legs and saunter along the front.

The idea for the railway stemmed from the difficulty the owners of the castle were having in persuading people to walk the 2 miles (3km) from the pier. A group of promoters was formed and surveying began. Part of the route uses an old carriage drive that was built in the 1850s between the castle and the pier but never used, because the Kirk refused to allow it to cross church land for the final part. The route was so overgrown with rhododendrons 120 years later that the survey had to be done on hands and knees. However, the colours in early summer are now one of the railway's attractions. The official opening by Chris Green, then the General Manager of ScotRail and now Chief Executive of Virgin Trains, was on June 22nd 1984.

In complete contrast to the secluded character of the carriage drive is the first section of the line, which enjoys spectacular views over the Sound of Mull to Ben Nevis, the Glencoe Hills and the Island of Lismore.

The flora of Mull is unique and the southeast corner where Mull Rail runs is particularly diverse, bordered by damp shady cliffs, open grassland, woodlands and the sea shore. As the plants do not all flower at the same time, they provide an ever-changing backdrop to the rail journey as the seasons unfold.

A stop at a loop named Tarmstedt is an opportunity for passengers to watch the engine take water. Its naming after a German town is due to a former owner of Torosay, who was also the first chairman of the Mull & West Highland; he began two escape attempts from a prison camp in Germany at that narrow gauge station – the second was successful.

The railway also has a link with the Puffing Billy Railway in Victoria, Australia. The search for a suitable prototype on which to base the Mull & West Highland's third locomotive ended with the plans of a tank engine used on Australia's best-known tourist railway. The result is now thought to be the largest tank engine of 10¼in (260mm) gauge in the world, which can haul 11 carriages with 190 passengers for the 20-minute journey.

ABOVE: OILING ROUND THE 2-6-4T, *LADY OF THE ISLES*.

LEFT: *LADY OF THE ISLES* STANDS READY TO DEPART AT CRAIGNURE WITH THE SOUND OF MULL AS A SCENIC BACKDROP.

FAR LEFT: DESPITE THE NARROWNESS OF ITS GAUGE, THE DELIGHTFUL MULL & WEST HIGHLAND RAILWAY PERFORMS AN IMPORTANT TRANSPORT TASK – TAKING VISITORS FROM THE FERRY PIER AT CRAIGNURE TO TOROSAY CASTLE.

Strathspey Railway

Highland

Aviemore, 29 miles (46.5km) south of Inverness

TRAIN SERVICE

DAILY FROM JUNE TO SEPTEMBER. LIMITED SERVICE IN APRIL, MAY AND OCTOBER. SANTA SPECIALS.

TEL: 01479 810725

WEBSITE: WWW.STRATHSPEYRAILWAY.CO.UK

This line follows the valley of the River Spey, with the Cairngorm Mountains rising to the southeast. Since the growth of winter sports in Scotland during the late 1960s, Aviemore has become the major centre for skiing, a network of chairlifts serving slopes around the small town. Until then it was known for little more than being an important junction on the railway between Perth and Inverness, where trains went either directly to Inverness over Slochd summit or took the circuitous route through Forres and Nairn. Passenger services over the latter were withdrawn in 1965, but preservationists and the Highlands & Islands Development Board wanted to save the 13-mile (21km) line between Aviemore and the historic town of Grantown-on-Spey.

Initial efforts came to fruition in 1978 when regular services were resumed during the tourist season between Aviemore and Boat of Garten. In 2002, an extra 4-mile (6.5km) section was opened as far as Broomhill leaving just 3 miles (5km) to be rebuilt to bring back trains to Grantown.

Strathspey Railway trains run into the main line station at Aviemore where connections can be made with ScotRail services to Inverness, Pitlochry, Perth, Stirling, Glasgow and Edinburgh. The Strathspey has one of the finest locomotive sheds on any preserved railway – a solid stone four track structure which became a garage after its closure in 1966. Now fully restored to its rightful use, it can be seen to the east as the train pulls out of Aviemore for the 40-minute journey to Broomhill.

Once over a level crossing serving the holiday village at Dalfaber, the line is into open country with fine views of the Cairngorm mountains to the east and the Monadhliaths to the west. Clumps of trees sometimes indicate remnants of the Caledonian Forest.

LEFT: LMS IVATT CLASS 2MT 2-6-0 NO. 46512 ON THE BANKS OF THE RIVER SPEY.

RIGHT AND TOP RIGHT: THIS BLUE CALEDONIAN RAILWAY GOODS ENGINE HAS BEEN RESTORED TO WORKING ORDER ON THE STRATHSPEY RAILWAY.

Silver birches accompany the approach to Boat of Garten, where it is worth spending some time. You can alight here, 15 minutes from Aviemore and catch a later train to complete the round trip of the line. The Strathspey Railway's excellent guide book suggests two walks from the station. An observation hide provided by the Royal Society for the Protection of Birds overlooks Loch Garten and is 3 miles (5km) from the station. Since the 1950s, the loch has been home to Ospreys, which return here each year from their winter refuge in Africa. Beyond Boat of Garten the 'strath' (valley) opens out to give views of the River Spey and the Cairngorm Mountain range. About two-thirds of the way from Boat of Garten the embankment of the line to Craigellachie can be seen curving away to the east. From Broomhill there is a pleasant waymarked riverside walk to the village of Nethy Bridge, 1.25 miles (2km) away.

Miniature Railways

Four of Britain's longest miniature railways are featured separately, but there are dozens of other miniature railways, ranging from short end-to-end lines to complex interwoven railways with runs of a mile or more.

Examples of these masterpieces of compression may be found on the Forest Railroad at Dobwalls, where one of the largest steam locomotives ever built, the Union Pacific *Big Boy*, is reproduced for a 7¼in (184mm) gauge line. It takes several trips to fathom the layout, thanks to the ingenuity of its design. Footpaths take visitors to viewing points where a succession of US goliaths-in-miniature pass by with trains of 30–40 people. The Moors Valley Railway, in the country park near Ringwood, is equally ambitious. Of the same gauge, it gives the feel of a busy main line during holiday periods, when several trains are running and the signal boxes are necessary rather than just decorative. The main station has an overall roof that adds to the atmosphere of a main line in miniature, and doubles as a carriage shed.

The Conwy Valley Railway at Betws-y-Coed, and Gorse Blossom Farm railways both have delightful settings, in the latter case twisting through the Devonshire woodland in deep cuttings, tunnels or bridges. At Betws-y-Coed, the line runs parallel with the scenic main line from Llandudno Junction to Blaenau Ffestiniog, through the foothills of Snowdonia. The Audley End Railway in Essex is perhaps the best-known of a number of railways that operate at country houses, running on estate farmland so as not to detract from the garden. Another notable example, at Weston Park in Shropshire, features a viaduct over part of a lake.

The Fairbourne & Barmouth is probably the most original of the many seaside railways. Built on the route of a much older line, this unique 12¼in (311mm) line has some very fine models of narrow gauge prototypes running through tunnels amid the sand dunes of the Mawddach estuary. Another seaside line is Norfolk's Wells & Walsingham, built on the trackbed of a British Railways branch line, and providing a public transport link as well as a pleasurable ride.

ABOVE: AMERICAN-OUTLINE STEAM LOCOMOTIVES ARE IMPRESSIVELY LARGE EVEN WHEN SCALED DOWN.

Scotland's finest passenger carrying miniature railway is Kerr's 10¼in (260 mm) gauge system at Arbroath, complete with coal-fired live steam. Founded by Matthew Kerr in 1935, the system continues to be run by his son, also named Matthew. It is located on the A92 Angus Coastal Tourist Route. Arbroath is also famous for its 'smokies' (smoked haddock). The railway is open weekends April to September inclusive and daily July to mid-August. Tel: 01241 879249

An unusual line operates on Sundays during the summer for the benefit of charities. The Great Cockrow Railway at Chertsey in Surrey, was founded by the transport publisher Ian Allan and is run by a group of volunteers, rather like a standard gauge preserved railway. It has state-of-the-art electronic as well as mechanical signalling, which is vital for the safe control of four or five moving trains.

ABOVE: MANY MINIATURE LINES OPERATE NARROW-GAUGE OUTLINE LOCOMOTIVES TO GAIN MORE BOILER POWER RELATIVE TO THEIR SIZE.

LEFT: TWO MILLION PASSENGERS HAVE TRAVELLED ON KERR'S MINIATURE RAILWAY AT ARBROATH.

TOP LEFT: THE WELLS & WALSINGHAM RAILWAY CLAIMS TO BE THE LONGEST 10¼IN GAUGE RAILWAY IN THE WORLD.

Index